At Issue

Immigration Reform

Other Books in the At Issue Series

Are Graphic Music Lyrics Harmful?

Bilingual Education

Caffeine

Can Diets Be Harmful?

Childhood Obesity

Corporate Corruption

Does the Internet Increase Anxiety?

Foodborne Outbreaks

Foreign Oil Dependence

How Valuable Is a College Degree?

Invasive Species

The Olympics

Student Loans

Superbugs

Superfoods

Voter Fraud

What Is the Impact of Green Practices?

What Should We Eat?

At Issue

Immigration Reform

Noël Merino, Book Editor

GREENHAVEN PRESS
A part of Gale, Cengage Learning

GALE
CENGAGE Learning·

Farmington Hills, Mich • San Francisco • New York • Waterville, Maine
Meriden, Conn • Mason, Ohio • Chicago

Judy Galens, *Manager, Frontlist Acquisitions*

© 2016 Greenhaven Press, a part of Gale, Cengage Learning.

Gale and Greenhaven Press are registered trademarks used herein under license.

For more information, contact:
Greenhaven Press
27500 Drake Rd.
Farmington Hills, MI 48331-3535
Or you can visit our Internet site at gale.cengage.com

For product information and technology assistance, contact us at

Gale Customer Support, 1-800-877-4253
For permission to use material from this text or product, submit all requests online at www.cengage.com/permissions.

Further permissions questions can be e-mailed to permissionrequest@cengage.com.

Articles in Greenhaven Press anthologies are often edited for length to meet page requirements. In addition, original titles of these works are changed to clearly present the main thesis and to explicitly indicate the author's opinion. Every effort is made to ensure that Greenhaven Press accurately reflects the original intent of the authors. Every effort has been made to trace the owners of copyrighted material.

Cover photograph copyright © Images.com/Corbis.

LIBRARY OF CONGRESS CATALOGING-IN-PUBLICATION DATA

Names: Merino, Noël, editor.
Title: Immigration reform / Noël Merino, book editor.
Description: Farmington Hills, Mich : Greenhaven Press, a part of Gale, Cengage Learning, [2016] | Series: At issue | Includes bibliographical references and index.
Identifiers: LCCN 2015024202 | ISBN 9780737774023 (hardcover) | ISBN 9780737774030 (pbk.)
Subjects: LCSH: United States--Emigration and immigration--Government policy.
Classification: LCC JV6483 .I557 2016 | DDC 325.73--dc23
LC record available at http://lccn.loc.gov/2015024202

Printed in Mexico
1 2 3 4 5 6 7 19 18 17 16 15

Contents

Introduction   7

1. Unauthorized Immigrants: Who They Are   10
   and What the Public Thinks
   Pew Research Center

2. Executive Action on Immigration Is Necessary   16
   Barack Obama

3. Executive Action on Immigration Sets   24
   a Dangerous Precedent
   John G. Malcolm

4. Obama Has the Law—and Reagan—on His   31
   Side on Immigration
   Erwin Chemerinsky and Sam Kleiner

5. Crafting a Successful Legalization Program: 35
   Lessons from the Past
   Lisa S. Roney

6. Mass Legalization for Unauthorized   45
   Immigrants Is a Bad Idea
   American Immigration Control Foundation

7. Yes, Amnesty Encourages More   56
   Illegal Immigration
   Ian Smith

8. Legalization of Unauthorized Immigrants   60
   Would Benefit the US Economy
   *Marshall Fitz, Philip E. Wolgin, and Patrick
   Oakford*

9. Legalization of Unauthorized Immigrants   68
   Would Burden the US Economy
   Federation for American Immigration Reform

10. The Green Economy and a Path to Citizenship   **73**
    David Foster

11. A Path to Citizenship Should Not Be   **77**
    a Part of Immigration Reform
    Peter Skerry

12. Should There Be a Path to Citizenship?   **82**
    Mark Krikorian

13. Immigration Reform as a Path to Conscience,   **86**
    Not Just Citizenship
    Christian Science Monitor

14. A Guest-Worker Program Is the Best   **89**
    Immigration Reform
    Ben Carson

15. Amnesty Is the Only Feasible Solution   **93**
    to the Immigration Problem
    Ed Krayewski

Organizations to Contact   **97**

Bibliography   **103**

Index   **109**

Introduction

It is often said that the United States is a nation of immigrants, yet not all immigrants are legally permitted into the country. Anyone born in the United States is granted US citizenship. Immigrants can come to the United States legally by being granted permanent residence, being admitted as a refugee, or having authorized temporary residence for work or as a family member of an authorized worker. Permanent residents who meet certain requirements can go on to become US citizens if they wish, so-called naturalized citizens.

Unauthorized immigrants are foreign-born noncitizens who do not have the legal authority to be living in the United States. For many unauthorized immigrants, entrance to the United States was legal, granted through a work visa or a visitor visa; but once the visa expires, they are no longer authorized to live and work in the United States. For other unauthorized immigrants, they arrived by crossing the US border illegally, without a work or visitor visa. There are millions of unauthorized immigrants currently living and often working in the United States: estimates vary, but most put the figure at a minimum of eleven million.

The question of how the United States should reform current immigration policy is full of controversy. There are two key issues to address: first, any reform must decide what to do about these millions of immigrants in the United States illegally; second, there is the question of what policies ought to guide immigration in the future. In debating these issues, it is invariably pointed out that the United States already dealt with these same questions in the 1980s.

The Immigration Reform and Control Act (IRCA) was passed by Congress and signed into law by President Ronald Reagan in 1986. At the time, President Reagan said, "Future generations of Americans will be thankful for our efforts to humanely regain control of our borders and thereby preserve the value of one of the most sacred possessions of our people, American citizenship." At the time, it was estimated that there were approximately five million unauthorized immigrants in the United States. IRCA allowed a process whereby certain unauthorized immigrants residing in the United States at that time could obtain legal permanent residence, with the possibility of obtaining citizenship later. IRCA attempted to halt unlawful immigration by enacting sanctions for employers who knowingly hire unauthorized immigrants and by requiring employers to attest to their employees' legal immigration status. It also attempted to meet the needs of employers by legalizing certain seasonal agricultural workers.

The most controversial part of IRCA was the so-called amnesty provision—the granting of legal permanent residence to immigrants residing and working in the United States without legal permission. This was supposed to be a one-time occurrence, with the other components of the law intended to prevent further unauthorized immigration. About half of the unauthorized immigrants residing in the United States did obtain legal status from IRCA. On the whole, however, IRCA did not halt unlawful immigration, and over a quarter-century later there are more than eleven million unauthorized immigrants in the United States—more than double the number that existed at the time that IRCA was passed.

The competing viewpoints on the issue of current immigration reform often point to IRCA but with different conclusions for future policy. David North of the Center for Immigration Studies says of the permanent residency granted to unauthorized immigrants—the so-called amnesty provision—in the 1986 IRCA:

We should never have another broad-brush amnesty. Such programs swell our already over-swollen population with still more low-income, lightly educated people and encourage future legal and illegal immigration, and thus create arguments for future amnesties.[1]

But others claim that IRCA amnesty was not what caused further illegal immigration. Philip E. Wolgin and Abhay Aneja at the Center for American Progress argue, "The problem with IRCA was not the legalization component; it was the lack of an extant enforcement apparatus and a failure to produce a vision for future migration."[2] What is clear is that opinion about the 1986 IRCA affects one's viewpoint on current immigration reform.

The issue of immigration in the United States has long been a source of controversy and continues to be so today. In *At Issue: Immigration Reform*, authors put forth a variety of viewpoints in the debate over immigration reform. The divergent viewpoints of this volume illustrate that there is wide disagreement about how to move forward with immigration policy in the United States.

Notes

1. David North, "Before Considering Another Amnesty, Look at IRCA's Lessons," Center for Immigration Studies, January 2013. www.cis.org/before-considering -another-amnesty-look-at-ircas-lessons.

2. Philip E. Wolgin and Abhay Aneja, "The Top 5 Reasons Why Immigration Reform in 2013 Is Different Than in 1986," Center for American Progress, June 12, 2013. www.americanprogress.org/issues/immigration/news/2013/06/12/66208 /the-top-5-reasons-why-immigration-reform-in-2013-is-different-than-in-1986.

1

Unauthorized Immigrants: Who They Are and What the Public Thinks

Pew Research Center

The Pew Research Center is a nonpartisan fact tank that informs the public about the issues, attitudes, and trends shaping America and the world.

The American public is divided on what to do about the more than eleven million unauthorized immigrants—about half of whom are from Mexico—in the United States. Most Americans support a way for unauthorized immigrants to gain legal status if they meet certain requirements, but the public is divided on President Barack Obama's recent executive action expanding the number of unauthorized immigrants permitted to stay and work in the United States.

The U.S. is a nation of immigrants. But unauthorized immigrants and U.S. immigration policy have become a source of political debate, with Congress and President Obama disagreeing over the best course of action to address issues such as deportations, shielding unauthorized immigrants from deportation, securing the border, and overhauling the nation's legal immigration system. That debate comes as the U.S. marks the 50th anniversary of the 1965 Immigration Act that has provided the foundation of today's immigration laws.

For years, the Pew Research Center has estimated the size and characteristics of the U.S. unauthorized immigrant population and surveyed Americans about immigration policy. Here are key findings.

Americans are divided over the executive action President Obama announced last November expanding the number of undocumented immigrants permitted to work and stay in the U.S.

About as many disapprove (50%) as approve (46%) of Obama's action, which could make up to 4 million people newly eligible for deportation relief, according to a survey last December. About eight-in-ten Republicans (82%) disapprove of the executive action and about seven-in-ten Democrats (72%) approve of it, with very strong attitudes on both sides. Hispanics overwhelmingly support the deportation-relief action: 81% approve, including 59% who very strongly approve. But non-Hispanic whites disapprove of it by nearly two-to-one (62% vs. 34%), with nearly half (49%) disapproving very strongly.

Mexico has been the top source of the number of unauthorized immigrants since at least 1995, and today accounts for about half the total.

Unauthorized immigrants from Mexico will benefit most under Obama's executive actions.

According to a Pew Research analysis, 44% of unauthorized immigrants from Mexico could apply for deportation protection under the new programs, compared with 24% of those from other parts of the world. The largest group who stand to benefit—at least 3.5 million, according to estimates of 2012 data—consists of unauthorized immigrant parents who have lived in the U.S. for at least five years and have children who either were born in the U.S. or are legal permanent residents.

There were 11.2 million unauthorized Immigrants In the U.S. as of 2012.

The total number of unauthorized immigrants living in the U.S. has not changed since 2009, standing at 11.2 million in 2012. *(A preliminary Pew Research estimate put the 2013 population of unauthorized immigrants at 11.3 million, statistically unchanged from the 2012 figure.)* Before then, the unauthorized immigration population had risen rapidly, from 3.5 million in 1990 to a peak of 12.2 million in 2007, the year that the Great Recession began. Another major trend has been the decline in the number of unauthorized immigrants from Mexico, falling to 5.9 million in 2012 from a peak of 6.9 million in 2007.

About half of the unauthorized immigrant population in the U.S. comes from Mexico.

Mexico has been the top source of the number of unauthorized immigrants since at least 1995, and today accounts for about half the total. Ranking second is El Salvador (675,000 in 2012), followed by Guatemala (525,000), India (450,000), Honduras (350,000), China (300,000) and the Philippines (200,000). But largely because of a marked decline in Mexican unauthorized immigrants since 2009, the shares of unauthorized immigrants from other nations and regions have grown. The sudden reversal of a long trend of growth in the number of Mexican unauthorized immigrants probably results from both a marked decline in new arrivals and an increase in departures to Mexico.

While the number of unauthorized immigrants leveled off nationally from 2009 to 2012, there were increases in seven states and declines in 14.

Six states—California, Texas, Florida, New York, New Jersey and Illinois—accounted for 60% of unauthorized immigrants in 2012. But illustrating the shifting trends in immigration patterns within the U.S., five East Coast states were among those seeing increases in the number of unauthorized immigrants from 2009 to 2012: Florida, Maryland, New Jersey, Pennsylvania and Virginia. Meanwhile, the unauthorized immigrant population declined in six Western states, including California and Nevada, which have been popular destinations for those immigrants. In 13 of the 14 states where there were declines in the unauthorized immigrant population, the chief factor was the drop in the number of unauthorized immigrants from Mexico.

Most Americans support a way for unauthorized immigrants to gain legal status if they meet certain requirements.

Seven-in-ten Americans support a way for undocumented immigrants to gain legal status if certain requirements are met. Most of those who support legal status think there should be a way for unauthorized immigrants to become citizens (43% overall), while 24% say the path should only include permanent residency. About eight-in-ten (83%) Democrats favor a pathway to legal status compared with 53% of Republicans. Majorities of blacks (75%) and whites (64%) continue to say undocumented immigrants should be allowed to stay in the U.S. legally if certain requirements are met. And about nine-in-ten (92%) Hispanics continue to support a pathway to legal status.

Republicans are more likely to say tougher law enforcement and stepped up border security is the top priority. Democrats are more likely to favor putting equal priority on tougher enforcement as well as finding a way for those in the U.S. illegally to become citizens.

About four-in-ten (41%) Americans said in an August 2014 survey that equal priority should be given to providing a path to citizenship for those here illegally *and* to better border security and enforcement, while 33% put the emphasis on tougher enforcement and 23% prioritized the pathway to citizenship. About half (53%) of Republicans said the priority should be tougher border controls and enforcement while just 36% favored equal emphasis on both priorities. In contrast,

45% of Democrats favored equal emphasis on both priorities while 33% said the focus should be on finding a way for those here illegally to become citizens if they meet certain requirements. Among Latino registered voters, 84% said in a Sept.–Oct. survey that creating a pathway to citizenship for undocumented immigrants should either be the top priority (46%) or just as important as better border security (38%).

Among Latino registered voters, 51% say deportation relief is more important than a pathway to citizenship for undocumented immigrants.

U.S. deportations of immigrants reached a record high in 2013.

The Obama administration deported a record 438,421 unauthorized immigrants in fiscal year 2013, continuing a streak of stepped up enforcement that has resulted in more than 2 million deportations since Obama took office, according to Department of Homeland Security data. Up to that point, the current administration deported about as many immigrants in five years as the George W. Bush administration deported in eight years. A survey conducted in February found the public evenly divided over whether the increase in deportations was a good or a bad thing.

U.S. Hispanics say relief from the threat of deportation is more important than a pathway to citizenship.

Among U.S. Hispanics, a larger share—by 56% to 35%— said in a Sept.–Oct. 2014 survey that it is more important that unauthorized immigrants be able to live and work in the U.S. without threat of deportation than have a pathway to citizenship. Among Hispanic adults, immigrants (59%) are more likely than U.S.-born Hispanics (54%) to say that being able to live and work legally is more important. Among Latino registered voters, 51% say deportation relief is more important than a pathway to citizenship for undocumented immigrants. Meanwhile, four-in-ten Latino voters say the opposite.

In a 2013 survey, 46% of Hispanics said they worried "a lot" (25%) or "some" (21%) that they themselves, a family member or a close friend could be deported.

As the number of unauthorized immigrants levels off, those who remain in the country are more likely to be long-term residents and live with their U.S.-born children.

Among the nation's 10.4 million unauthorized adults, a shrinking share have been in the country for less than five years—15% in 2012, compared with 38% in 2000. A rising share have lived in the U.S. for a decade or more—62% in 2012, compared with 35% in 2000. About a fifth (21%) have been in the U.S. for two decades or more, as of 2012.

Children with at least one unauthorized immigrant parent made up 6.9% of students enrolled in kindergarten through 12th grade in the U.S.

Among elementary and secondary school students with unauthorized immigrant parents, the U.S.-born share has grown since 2007 while the share who are themselves unauthorized immigrants has declined. Most (5.5% of all students) are U.S.-born children who are U.S. citizens at birth. The rest (1.4%) are unauthorized immigrants themselves.

Unauthorized immigrants account for one-in-twenty people in the U.S. workforce.

Unauthorized immigrants accounted for one-in-twenty people in the labor force, or 8.1 million people in 2012, but the share is markedly higher in some states, especially those with high shares of unauthorized immigrants in the population (like Nevada, California and Texas).

2

Executive Action on Immigration Is Necessary

Barack Obama

Barack Obama is the forty-fourth president of the United States.

The United States has a broken immigration system and three actions on the issue will provide a temporary solution until Congress can get a bill passed. The immigration system will be reformed to increase border security, simplify immigration for high-skilled immigrants, and temporarily stop deportation of certain unauthorized immigrants. We are a nation of immigrants and it is not reasonable or fair to think that the current system can be reformed without allowing many already here the option to stay.

For more than 200 years, our tradition of welcoming immigrants from around the world has given us a tremendous advantage over other nations. It's kept us youthful, dynamic, and entrepreneurial. It has shaped our character as a people with limitless possibilities—people not trapped by our past, but able to remake ourselves as we choose.

A Broken Immigration System

But today, our immigration system is broken—and everybody knows it.

Families who enter our country the right way and play by the rules watch others flout the rules. Business owners who

Barack Obama, Remarks by the President in Address to the Nation on Immigration, White House, November 20, 2014.

offer their workers good wages and benefits see the competition exploit undocumented immigrants by paying them far less. All of us take offense to anyone who reaps the rewards of living in America without taking on the responsibilities of living in America. And undocumented immigrants who desperately want to embrace those responsibilities see little option but to remain in the shadows, or risk their families being torn apart.

It's been this way for decades. And for decades, we haven't done much about it.

When I took office, I committed to fixing this broken immigration system. And I began by doing what I could to secure our borders. Today, we have more agents and technology deployed to secure our southern border than at any time in our history. And over the past six years, illegal border crossings have been cut by more than half. Although this summer [2014], there was a brief spike in unaccompanied children being apprehended at our border, the number of such children is now actually lower than it's been in nearly two years. Overall, the number of people trying to cross our border illegally is at its lowest level since the 1970s. Those are the facts.

Our law enforcement personnel . . . can stem the flow of illegal crossings, and speed the return of those who do cross over.

An Unpassed Bill

Meanwhile, I worked with Congress on a comprehensive fix, and last year, 68 Democrats, Republicans, and independents came together to pass a bipartisan bill in the Senate. It wasn't perfect. It was a compromise. But it reflected common sense. It would have doubled the number of border patrol agents while giving undocumented immigrants a pathway to citizenship if they paid a fine, started paying their taxes, and went to the back of the line. And independent experts said that it would help grow our economy and shrink our deficits.

Had the House of Representatives allowed that kind of bill a simple yes-or-no vote, it would have passed with support from both parties, and today it would be the law. But for a year and a half now, Republican leaders in the House have refused to allow that simple vote.

Now, I continue to believe that the best way to solve this problem is by working together to pass that kind of common sense law. But until that happens, there are actions I have the legal authority to take as President—the same kinds of actions taken by Democratic and Republican presidents before me—that will help make our immigration system more fair and more just.

Tonight, I am announcing those actions.

First, we'll build on our progress at the border with additional resources for our law enforcement personnel so that they can stem the flow of illegal crossings, and speed the return of those who do cross over.

Second, I'll make it easier and faster for high-skilled immigrants, graduates, and entrepreneurs to stay and contribute to our economy, as so many business leaders have proposed.

Third, we'll take steps to deal responsibly with the millions of undocumented immigrants who already live in our country.

The Deal for Undocumented Immigrants

I want to say more about this third issue, because it generates the most passion and controversy. Even as we are a nation of immigrants, we're also a nation of laws. Undocumented workers broke our immigration laws, and I believe that they must be held accountable—especially those who may be dangerous. That's why, over the past six years, deportations of criminals are up 80 percent. And that's why we're going to keep focusing enforcement resources on actual threats to our security. Felons, not families. Criminals, not children. Gang members, not a mom who's working hard to provide for her kids. We'll prioritize, just like law enforcement does every day.

But even as we focus on deporting criminals, the fact is, millions of immigrants in every state, of every race and nationality still live here illegally. And let's be honest—tracking down, rounding up, and deporting millions of people isn't realistic. Anyone who suggests otherwise isn't being straight with you. It's also not who we are as Americans. After all, most of these immigrants have been here a long time. They work hard, often in tough, low-paying jobs. They support their families. They worship at our churches. Many of their kids are American-born or spent most of their lives here, and their hopes, dreams, and patriotism are just like ours. As my predecessor, President [George W.] Bush, once put it: "They are a part of American life."

Now here's the thing: We expect people who live in this country to play by the rules. We expect that those who cut the line will not be unfairly rewarded. So we're going to offer the following deal: If you've been in America for more than five years; if you have children who are American citizens or legal residents; if you register, pass a criminal background check, and you're willing to pay your fair share of taxes—you'll be able to apply to stay in this country temporarily without fear of deportation. You can come out of the shadows and get right with the law. That's what this deal is.

Now, let's be clear about what it isn't. This deal does not apply to anyone who has come to this country recently. It does not apply to anyone who might come to America illegally in the future. It does not grant citizenship, or the right to stay here permanently, or offer the same benefits that citizens receive—only Congress can do that. All we're saying is we're not going to deport you.

A Temporary Solution

I know some of the critics of this action call it amnesty. Well, it's not. Amnesty is the immigration system we have today—millions of people who live here without paying their taxes or playing by the rules while politicians use the issue to scare people and whip up votes at election time.

That's the real amnesty—leaving this broken system the way it is. Mass amnesty would be unfair. Mass deportation would be both impossible and contrary to our character. What I'm describing is accountability—a common-sense, middle-ground approach: If you meet the criteria, you can come out of the shadows and get right with the law. If you're a criminal, you'll be deported. If you plan to enter the U.S. illegally, your chances of getting caught and sent back just went up.

The actions I'm taking are not only lawful, they're the kinds of actions taken by every single Republican President and every single Democratic President for the past half century. And to those members of Congress who question my authority to make our immigration system work better, or question the wisdom of me acting where Congress has failed, I have one answer: Pass a bill.

Our history and the facts show that immigrants are a net plus for our economy and our society.

I want to work with both parties to pass a more permanent legislative solution. And the day I sign that bill into law, the actions I take will no longer be necessary. Meanwhile, don't let a disagreement over a single issue be a dealbreaker on every issue. That's not how our democracy works, and Congress certainly shouldn't shut down our government again just because we disagree on this. Americans are tired of gridlock. What our country needs from us right now is a common purpose—a higher purpose.

Most Americans support the types of reforms I've talked about tonight. But I understand the disagreements held by many of you at home. Millions of us, myself included, go back generations in this country, with ancestors who put in the painstaking work to become citizens. So we don't like the notion that anyone might get a free pass to American citizenship.

I know some worry immigration will change the very fabric of who we are, or take our jobs, or stick it to middle-class families at a time when they already feel like they've gotten the raw deal for over a decade. I hear these concerns. But that's not what these steps would do. Our history and the facts show that immigrants are a net plus for our economy and our society. And I believe it's important that all of us have this debate without impugning each other's character.

Who We Are as a Nation

Because for all the back and forth of Washington, we have to remember that this debate is about something bigger. It's about who we are as a country, and who we want to be for future generations.

Are we a nation that tolerates the hypocrisy of a system where workers who pick our fruit and make our beds never have a chance to get right with the law? Or are we a nation that gives them a chance to make amends, take responsibility, and give their kids a better future?

Are we a nation that accepts the cruelty of ripping children from their parents' arms? Or are we a nation that values families, and works together to keep them together?

Are we a nation that educates the world's best and brightest in our universities, only to send them home to create businesses in countries that compete against us? Or are we a nation that encourages them to stay and create jobs here, create businesses here, create industries right here in America?

That's what this debate is all about. We need more than politics as usual when it comes to immigration. We need reasoned, thoughtful, compassionate debate that focuses on our hopes, not our fears. I know the politics of this issue are tough. But let me tell you why I have come to feel so strongly about it.

Over the past few years, I have seen the determination of immigrant fathers who worked two or three jobs without taking a dime from the government, and at risk any moment of losing it all, just to build a better life for their kids. I've seen the heartbreak and anxiety of children whose mothers might be taken away from them just because they didn't have the right papers. I've seen the courage of students who, except for the circumstances of their birth, are as American as Malia or Sasha [daughters of Barack and Michelle Obama]; students who bravely come out as undocumented in hopes they could make a difference in the country they love.

These people—our neighbors, our classmates, our friends—they did not come here in search of a free ride or an easy life. They came to work, and study, and serve in our military, and above all, contribute to America's success.

An Immigrant Story

Tomorrow, I'll travel to Las Vegas and meet with some of these students, including a young woman named Astrid Silva. Astrid was brought to America when she was four years old. Her only possessions were a cross, her doll, and the frilly dress she had on. When she started school, she didn't speak any English. She caught up to other kids by reading newspapers and watching PBS [Public Broadcasting Service], and she became a good student. Her father worked in landscaping. Her mom cleaned other people's homes. They wouldn't let Astrid apply to a technology magnet school, not because they didn't love her, but because they were afraid the paperwork would out her as an undocumented immigrant—so she applied behind their back and got in. Still, she mostly lived in the shadows—until her grandmother, who visited every year from Mexico, passed away, and she couldn't travel to the funeral without risk of being found out and deported. It was around that time she decided to begin advocating for herself and others like her, and today, Astrid Silva is a college student working on her third degree.

Are we a nation that kicks out a striving, hopeful immigrant like Astrid, or are we a nation that finds a way to welcome her in? Scripture tells us that we shall not oppress a stranger, for we know the heart of a stranger—we were strangers once, too.

My fellow Americans, we are and always will be a nation of immigrants. We were strangers once, too. And whether our forebears were strangers who crossed the Atlantic, or the Pacific, or the Rio Grande, we are here only because this country welcomed them in, and taught them that to be an American is about something more than what we look like, or what our last names are, or how we worship. What makes us Americans is our shared commitment to an ideal—that all of us are created equal, and all of us have the chance to make of our lives what we will.

That's the country our parents and grandparents and generations before them built for us. That's the tradition we must uphold. That's the legacy we must leave for those who are yet to come.

3

Executive Action on Immigration Sets a Dangerous Precedent

John G. Malcolm

John G. Malcolm is director of the Edwin Meese III Center for Legal and Judicial Studies and the Ed Gilbertson and Sherry Lindberg Gilbertson Senior Legal Fellow at The Heritage Foundation.

President Barack Obama's 2014 executive action on immigration oversteps his authority, which he himself had noted on several occasions prior to the action. The president of the United States has limited authority over domestic issues, especially when Congress has made a decision on an issue; and in this case Congress declined to take action on the immigration law that President Obama wanted. Such action relies on a dangerous rationale that a president may take action whenever he or she wants.

It is no secret that President [Barack] Obama is a supporter of the DREAM [Development, Relief, and Education for Alien Minors] Act—legislation that has been debated and rejected numerous times by Congress. Yet, instead of doing the tough work of building trust, engaging in intense negotiating, and making compromises in search of a bipartisan solution, the President has decided to "go it alone" by implementing broad swathes of that proposed act by fiat. Setting aside the

John G. Malcolm, "President Obama's Executive Action on Immigration Sets a Dangerous Precedent," *Issue Brief*, no. 4313, Heritage Foundation, December 5, 2014, pp. 1–4.

substance of the President's policies, which others have effectively addressed, this unilateral approach is wrong and sets a dangerous precedent.

Limited Authority over Domestic Affairs

While the President has broad authority when acting as the "Commander in Chief" in the areas of foreign affairs and national security, he has more limited authority with regard to domestic affairs, particularly when Congress has spoken on a particular issue. Indeed, prior to implementing his current [November 2014] plan, even the President acknowledged that he lacked the constitutional authority to engage in this executive action. For example, when speaking on this topic in 2011 to the National Council of La Raza (a group of Hispanic activists), President Obama said:

> The idea of doing things on my own is very tempting, I promise you, not just on immigration reform. But that's not how our system works. That's not how our democracy functions. That's not how our Constitution is written.

The President has been vested with executive authority. . . . He does not get to exercise legislative authority.

Additionally, in a March 2011 Univision Town Hall, President Obama was asked whether he would grant "temporary protected status" to undocumented students. He responded that:

> There are enough laws on the books by Congress that are very clear in terms of how we have to enforce our immigration system that for me to simply through executive order ignore those congressional mandates would not conform with my appropriate role as President.

And in February 2013, during a Google Hangout session, President Obama said:

The problem is that you know I'm the president of the United States. I'm not the emperor of the United States. My job is to execute laws that are passed, and Congress right now has not changed what I consider to be a broken immigration system. And what that means is that we have certain obligations to enforce the laws that are in place, even if we think that in many cases the results may be tragic.

President Obama is now arguing, "If you don't want me to take executive action, then just send me a bill that I like." Congress, however, has the right, if it wants to, to say, "No, we won't. Too darn bad."

Legal Precedent on the Issue

If the President let it be known that he thought that federal judges were being too harsh or too lenient in the sentences they gave, and if they refused to hand down sentences that he liked better, would the President have the right to start issuing sentences to criminal defendants? Of course not. The President has been vested with executive authority. He doesn't get to exercise judicial authority. And he does not get to exercise legislative authority either.

In the famous steel seizure case, *Youngstown Sheet & Tube Co. v. Sawyer*, the Supreme Court stated in no uncertain terms that the President's "power to see that the laws are faithfully executed refutes the idea that he is to be a lawmaker. . . . [T]he Constitution is neither silent nor equivocal about who shall make laws which the President is to execute." The separation of powers is one of this nation's core principles of governance. Although the President may not like congressional intransigence, at least as he sees it through his eyes, this does not give him the authority to act unilaterally.

The extent of the President's authority to ignore the will of Congress with respect to domestic policy has previously been considered by the Supreme Court. In *Train v. City of New York*, President Richard Nixon tried to impose his domestic priorities over the will of Congress by ignoring laws that Congress had passed. Nixon, desiring to cut the deficit and not wanting to fund certain programs he disliked (primarily environmental laws, farm programs, and subsidized housing), decided to impound funds dedicated to those programs. Congress reacted by enacting the Impoundment Control Act of 1974, which ordered the President to spend appropriated funds as directed by Congress.

This was challenged in court, and ultimately, a unanimous Supreme Court held that the President could not frustrate the will of Congress by killing a program through impoundment. Specifically, the Court determined that the President must carry out all of the objectives and the full scope of programs for which budget authority is provided by Congress.

What President Obama is doing with regard to immigration law has nothing to do with responding to a natural disaster, civil strife, political persecution, or foreign affairs.

A Duty to Enforce the Law

Article 1, Section 8 of the Constitution gives Congress exclusive authority to "establish a uniform Rule of Naturalization. . . ." The Supreme Court, in *Immigration and Naturalization Service v. Chadha*, clearly stated that "[t]he plenary authority of Congress over aliens under Art. I, § 8, cl. 4, is not open to question. . . ." This determination was reiterated in *Arizona v. United States*, when the Court held that Congress could trump state laws dealing with illegal aliens through the preemption doctrine but competing executive branch enforcement priorities could not.

The President's constitutional duty to enforce the laws derives from Art. II, sec. 3, which states that the President "shall take Care that the laws be faithfully executed." This is imperative language: It instructs that the President "shall take Care," not "take Care if he feels like it." His duty is to execute "the laws"—not some of the laws, not just the ones the President likes, but all of the laws. And he has to "faithfully" execute those laws.

Citing a memorandum from the Department of Justice's Office of Legal Counsel, the President has said that his actions are grounded in the executive's inherent authority to exercise prosecutorial discretion. Prosecutorial discretion with respect to an executive's enforcement duties is based on equitable considerations in an individual case or a small set of cases.

Yet the Immigration and Nationality Act of 1952 already provides authority for many equitable exceptions. For instance, U.S. immigration laws permit asylum or "Temporary Protected Status" for those who will, if returned to their home country, be subjected to hardships from civil war or natural disasters or those who will be subjected to persecution because of race, religion, nationality, membership in a particular social group, or political opinion. These are all exceptions that Congress created based on special considerations, that can be taken into account in particular cases, and which fulfill the objectives of our nation's immigration laws.

What President Obama is doing with regard to immigration law has nothing to do with responding to a natural disaster, civil strife, political persecution, or foreign affairs and everything to do with a disagreement with Congress about domestic immigration policy. He is implementing by executive fiat a policy—based on his policy preferences—that exempts a huge class of people from a law's applicability, against the will of Congress.

Kings and dictators give themselves the authority to grant dispensations, to determine, based on benevolence, a whim, a bribe, or perceived political advantage, that the law will not apply to certain favored individuals. Presidents do not have that authority.

Furthermore, prosecutorial discretion is designed to help achieve statutory objectives—which in this case would include promoting the integrity of the U.S. legal immigration system and deterring violations of our immigration laws—not to frustrate statutory objectives or to effectuate a change in policy.

A Dangerous Rationale

As former Immigration and Naturalization Service Commissioner Doris Meissner, who served under President Bill Clinton, once stated, prosecutorial discretion should not become "an invitation to violate or ignore the law." But that is exactly what the President's actions will do.

The President has essentially announced that roughly half of the illegal immigrants in this country, if you include those covered by the President's 2012 Deferred Action for Childhood Arrivals (DACA) policy—clear lawbreakers—have nothing to worry about. The President has encouraged them to "come out of the shadows"—guaranteeing that the immigration laws will not be applied to them and that they will, in fact, be given work permits.

The President has turned the notion of prosecutorial discretion upside down. Under normal circumstances, the law applies to everyone; prosecutorial discretion applies only in exceptional circumstances. With regard to immigration reform, the President has announced that the law will not apply to an extremely large group of people, but that it might apply to someone in that group based on exceptional circumstances—an ephemeral theoretical possibility if there ever was one.

This rationale may end up squeaking by in a court of law, assuming it is challenged by a plaintiff who is able to establish the legal requirements of standing, but it is too cute by half. This sleight of hand may be many things, but it is not the "faithful execution" of our immigration laws, and it is not a proper exercise of prosecutorial discretion.

In his concurring opinion in the *Youngstown Steel* case, Justice Felix Frankfurter wrote that "[t]he accretion of dangerous power does not come in a day. It does come, however slowly, from the generative force of unchecked disregard of the restrictions that fence in even the most disinterested assertion of authority." By taking such unprecedented unilateral action, the President has established a dangerous precedent that violates fundamental principles of separation of powers—those Founding ideals that established a government of laws and not of men and continue to serve as a bulwark, protecting Americans' liberties.

4

Obama Has the Law— and Reagan—on His Side on Immigration

Erwin Chemerinsky and Sam Kleiner

Erwin Chemerinsky is the dean and a distinguished professor of law at University of California, Irvine School of Law. Sam Kleiner is a fellow at the Yale Law Information Society Project.

The president of the United States has authority to decide whether or not the Department of Justice should enforce a certain law. This prosecutorial discretion is especially strong with respect to immigration since immigration is part of the nation's foreign affairs, an area of presidential authority. In fact, several past presidents have taken executive action in order to limit deportations for humanitarian reasons and President Barack Obama's executive action halting deportation can also be justified on humanitarian grounds.

President Obama is soon expected to take a step toward fixing our broken immigration system by issuing an executive order to halt deportations of undocumented immigrants whose children are U.S. citizens. Republicans, including Speaker of the House John Boehner and new Senate Majority Leader Mitch McConnell, have threatened reprisals against such an order. But one thing is clear: The president has the constitutional authority to decide to not proceed with deportations. It has always been within the president's discretion to decide whether to have the Department of Justice enforce a particular law. As the Supreme Court declared in *United States v. Nixon*, "the Executive Branch has exclusive authority and absolute discretion to decide whether to prosecute a case."

A president may choose to not enforce particular laws when deciding how to allocate scarce resources or based on his view of the best public policy. Few object, for example, when the Department of Justice does not prosecute those who possess small amounts of marijuana, even though they violated the federal Controlled Substance Act. There are countless federal laws that go unenforced. In 1800, then congressman and later Chief Justice John Marshall stated, the president may "direct that the criminal be prosecuted no further" because it is "the exercise of an indubitable and constitutional power."

The president's broad prosecutorial discretion has been repeatedly recognized by the courts. In 2013, Judge Brett Kavanaugh of the D.C. Circuit, appointed by George W. Bush, offered a strong defense: "The president may decline to prosecute certain violators of federal law just as the president may pardon certain violators of federal law," Judge Kavanaugh wrote. "The president may decline to prosecute or may pardon because of the president's own constitutional concerns about a law or because of policy objections to the law, among other reasons."

The [George W.] Bush administration explicitly recognized that humanitarian factors must play into the deportation decision.

This prosecutorial discretion is even greater in immigration because the treatment of foreign citizens is inextricably intertwined with the nation's foreign affairs, an area especially under the president's control. For example, the Supreme Court's decision in 2010 to overturn large parts of Arizona's restrictive immigration law, SB1070, was premised on the executive branch's need for discretion in the immigration context. "A principal feature of the removal system is the broad discretion exercised by immigration officials," the Court wrote, adding that "[t]he dynamic nature of relations with other countries requires the Executive Branch to ensure that enforcement policies are consistent with this Nation's foreign policy with respect to these and other realities." In a similar 1941 case, *Hines v. Davidowitz*, the Supreme Court voided a Pennsylvania system of alien registration because "experience has shown that international controversies of the gravest moment, sometimes even leading to war, may arise from real or imagined wrongs to another's subjects inflicted, or permitted, by a government."

Indeed, presidents of both parties have tailored immigration policy to their own goals. In 1987, the Reagan administration took executive action to limit deportations for 200,000 Nicaraguan exiles, even those who had been turned down for asylum. Similarly, President George H.W. Bush in 1990 limited deportations of Chinese students and in 1991 kept hundreds of Kuwait citizens from being deported. President Bill Clinton regularly used his power of prosecutorial discretion to limit deportations; in 1993 he gave 18-month extensions to Salvadoran residents, in 1997 he limited deportations for Haitians, and in 1998 he limited deportations to Central American counties that had been devastated by hurricanes.

President George W. Bush also took major steps to limit deportations on humanitarian grounds. In 2001, he limited deportation of Salvadorian citizens at the request of the Salvadorian president who said that their remittances were a key part of their nation's economy. The Bush administration embraced prosecutorial discretion and ordered the consideration of factors such as whether a mom was nursing a child or whether an undocumented person was a U.S. military veteran in making the determination on whether to order a deportation.

The Bush administration explicitly recognized that humanitarian factors must play into the deportation decision. The 2005 Howard memorandum issued by Immigrations and Customs Enforcement (ICE) stated that "Prosecutorial discretion is a very significant tool . . . to deal with the difficult, complex and contradictory provisions of the immigration laws and cases involving human suffering and hardship." Today, the Obama administration can build on that to stop deportations that separate parents from their children. The breaking up of families due to deportations undoubtedly causes human suffering and hardship: The Applied Research Center in its "Shattered Families" report found that over 5,000 children live in U.S. foster homes because their parents were deported.

The federal courts, too, have recognized that presidents inherently have the power to choose not to enforce immigration laws in a particular instance and thus to not initiate deportation proceedings even when a person is not lawfully in the country. In a famous case involving John Lennon, the United States Court of Appeals for the District of Columbia Circuit held that the president could issue an "an informal administrative stay of deportation" to allow Lennon to remain in the country. The case, *INS v. Lennon*, allowed the executive branch to halt the deportation of Lennon and expressly recognized president's constitutional power to exercise prosecutorial discretion in the immigration context.

The president clearly has the power to limit deportation of an individual or a group of individuals, even a large group. Such action does not grant citizenship to the undocumented; it merely is a temporary measure that halts deportations. It is not a permanent fix to the intractable challenge of how to deal with undocumented immigration, but it is increasingly looking like the only solution that the president has in facing an intransigent Congress that is unwilling to act.

5

Crafting a Successful Legalization Program: Lessons from the Past

Lisa S. Roney

Lisa S. Roney retired in 2009 as director of the Research and Evaluation Division of the Office of Policy and Strategy at US Citizenship and Immigration Services (USCIS).

With immigration reform, a new legalization program needs to be crafted with lessons from the past Immigration Reform Control Act of 1986 in mind. Any new legalization program needs to be simple and efficient, inclusive, affordable, safe, promote administrative efficiency and manageability, and have all parts of the system work together. A new legalization program with these principles can avoid the pitfalls of the 1986 legalization program.

One of the themes that emerged from the Senate Judiciary Committee mark up of the 2013 Senate immigration bill was the necessity of avoiding the mistakes of the past. In the context of legalization for the 11 million unauthorized immigrants now in the United States, the argument is often made that the 1986 law wasn't tough enough, and any new legalization program should have more requirements and restrictions. However, in my 39-year career with the Department of Homeland Security (DHS) and former Immigration and Naturalization Service (INS), and after years of studying implementation of the 1986 law, I've reached a different conclusion. A successful legalization program depends on simplicity and common sense. There are many lessons to be learned from the 1986 law about how to design a better legalization program. Fortunately, many of those lessons have been absorbed by the drafters of S. 744, the Border Security, Economic Opportunity and Immigration Modernization Act. Nonetheless, as the debate continues on this bill, it is important to reiterate the importance of good design and thoughtful implementation. That is what will ensure success and provide the country with a working immigration system.

This essay reinforces the importance of the lessons learned from IRCA, the Immigration Reform Control Act of 1986— and the necessity for adhering to them as debate on immigration reform continues. Lessons from the past for designing a new legalization program can be categorized into six basic principles: keep it simple, be inclusive, make it affordable, make it safe, promote administrative efficiency, and make all parts of the system work together.

Principle 1: Keep the Program Simple

The simplest and most efficient legalization program would be a single-application process resulting in immediate permanent resident status. However, because unauthorized immigrants have been living outside the legal system for many years and may need time to collect needed documentation and meet prospective program criteria (such as payment of penalties and acquiring English-language skills), this may be too large a step to take initially. Further, to the extent that legal status for some unauthorized immigrants is tied to the legal immigration process (where long waits may currently exist), that would leave many potential applicants without a legal status for many years, which would undermine the program by definition.

Based on experience with the 1986 legalization program, getting the unauthorized immigrant population registered and in lawful status quickly is the most important goal. Therefore, a two-stage program, similar to the 1986 legalization program, is desirable. Such a program would start with an initial registration period that grants temporary status, including employment authorization and permission to travel. This would attract the maximum number of unauthorized immigrants and get them on the path to qualifying for lawful permanent residence. The second stage of the program leading to permanent residence would include additional requirements such as payment of a penalty, proof of payment of assessed taxes, and acquisition of English-language skills. This stage would end with lawful permanent resident status for those successfully completing the process and, after an additional period of residence and meeting the criteria, could lead to U.S. citizenship.

The easier it is to demonstrate eligibility, the less . . . likely it is that applicants will have difficulty documenting their past residence and resort to use of fraudulent documentation.

Principle 2: Facilitate Inclusion

Participation

The provisions in IRCA required at least 5 years' residence to qualify, which created a significant documentary barrier for those who met the period-of-residence requirement but did not have the documents to prove it, and resulted in a significant population of residents who were left in unlawful status at the end of the program. A legalization program should be designed to allow the maximum number of unauthorized immigrants to participate. It is in the national interest to register all persons who are currently here in unlawful status so they are henceforth legally included in our society. A policy of inclusion entails provisions specifying a recent cut-off date and short period of continuous residence to qualify, as well as realistic and verifiable documentary requirements. Inclusion of the maximum number of unauthorized immigrants supports the first principle of keeping the program simple and prevents a residual unauthorized population.

Documentary Requirements

As shown in the 1986 program, the provisions for length of residence and documentary requirements are inherently intertwined; the longer the period of residence required and the earlier the cut-off date for residency, the more onerous the documentary requirements become to prove presence during this time. Conversely, the easier it is to demonstrate eligibility, the less difficult the administrative burden becomes to review documentation and the less likely it is that applicants will have difficulty documenting their past residence and resort to use of fraudulent documentation.

IRCA's provisions and its implementing regulations prudently facilitated the application process by not specifying the documentary requirements for proof of continuous residence. However, experience administering the 1986 program found that, because unauthorized immigrants seek to avoid detection, potentially changing employers and housing frequently, their lifestyles made them less likely to retain rent receipts, pay stubs, school records, and other evidence that could demonstrate continuous presence. Thus some qualified applicants used fraudulent documentation because it was their only option. Therefore, a recent cut-off date resulting in the need for less documentation reduces the burden on both applicants and the government to provide and review paperwork.

A policy of inclusion is strongly supported by the best studies of the unauthorized immigrant population, which estimate that most unauthorized immigrants have many years of residence in the United States. Nearly two-thirds have been here for at least 10 years; another 22 percent have been resident for 5 or more years, with only 15 percent having less than 5 years of residence. This population has the potential to be well on its way to being part of our society once allowed to come out of the shadows.

Inclusion of Spouses and Children

Unlike the 1986 legalization program, new legislation should provide derivative status for spouses and minor children of principal legalization applicants, whether inside or outside the United States. By excluding family members that did not qualify on their own merits, participation in the 1986 program was reduced, especially among those who were fearful that their family members might be deported. Moreover, following administrative attempts to provide status for immediate family members who did not qualify on their own, legislation was passed in 1990 to give provisional legal immigration status and work authorization to many of these family members. Doing so originally would have been far more efficient and humanitarian.

Designing the program to draw participants in voluntarily and encourage those who may be hesitant to apply is critical.

Data suggest that including the closest family members will not greatly increase numbers. Based in part on their relative youth, unauthorized immigrants are more likely to be living in nuclear families (with a spouse or cohabiting partner and children) than either legal-immigrant or U.S.-citizen adults. Overall, 45 percent of unauthorized immigrants live with a spouse or cohabitating partner and children, compared with 34 percent of legal-immigrant adults and 21 percent of U.S.-born adults. Currently, almost half of all unauthorized immigrants have minor U.S. children, the majority of whom are likely native-born U.S. citizens.

Length of Application Period

The initial process needs to be time limited but sufficiently long to register some 11 million unauthorized immigrants currently resident in the United States. Presumably, much—if not most—of the administrative legalization process, including intake, verification, adjudication, and notification, can be automated. The initial registration period for the 1986 legalization program was one year, which would presumably need to be extended to at least two years for the much larger number of applicants—the amount of time needed being offset by greater use of technology in a new program.

Designing the program to draw participants in voluntarily and encourage those who may be hesitant to apply is critical. Maintaining a steady flow of applications is also beneficial, since a more constant flow results in a better-administrated program. The IRCA legalization program saw a slow initial rise in applications at the beginning of the program as persons increasingly prepared their cases and saw that applying was safe. However, the initial period was followed by a drop in receipts midway through the program, with 30 percent of the applications filed in the last 2 months of the program, a time when funding levels and staffing were lower due to the reduced applications in the preceding months.

In addition to sufficient intake capacity, a publicity program needs to be funded to reach all groups of unauthorized immigrants regardless of their nationality or place of residence. During the 1986 legalization program, participation was uneven based on nationality and geographic area of the country, resulting in part from the level of publicity and languages and approaches used to reach the unauthorized population. Additionally, concerns about putting mixed-status family members at risk also reduced participation.

Criteria for Qualifying

Based on the 1986 program experiences, qualifications for the first temporary-resident phase should be kept to a minimum and include only passing a background check, proving identity, and having the requisite period of residence. By the time participants have reached the stage at which they are applying for permanent resident status, they should demonstrate that they have paid all assessed income taxes and either have sufficient English-language skills or be on a path to learning English. In both cases, however, those requirements must be reasonably designed for success. For instance, a "back taxes" requirement that requires compiling additional documents or endless hours at the IRS may impede efficient processing of applications. Similarly, advancing English proficiency requirements that are currently part of the naturalization process to the adjustment phase for legalization (something that has been proposed in the current Senate debate) extends processing times and ignores the limited resources often available to English language learners.

Grounds of exclusion applying to legalization applicants, as in the 1986 legalization program, must be appropriate to the process and be confined to those protecting the health, safety, security, and welfare of the United States. Grounds of exclusion applying to the 1986 cohort were limited to not having been convicted of a felony or three misdemeanors and not having persecuted anyone. Any minor infractions, including those committed at an early age, should be forgiven.

Principle 3: Make It Affordable

Fees and penalties should not deter participation in the program. The application fee should be meaningful, but within reach of participants, many of whom are living at or below the poverty level. As under the 1986 legalization program, the fee for families, including minor children, should be capped. However, the program should not be a financial burden on the nation; it should be largely self-funding, with fees covering most of the cost of the program. However, unlike the 1986 program, which was solely self-funded and reliant on the flow of applications, legislation should ensure appropriated funds for the start-up period and during and following slow application periods. Presumably, a majority of appropriated funds could be repaid into a fund to foster integration of applicants at the close of the program.

Administering a legalization program is a huge task, and a new program will pose a greater challenge than the 1986 program in terms of size.

It would be reasonable for any required monetary penalty to be paid at the time applicants adjust to permanent status, which would give participants in the temporary-registration phase time to acquire the amount of the penalty, including paying any assessed taxes and taking classes in English.

Principle 4: Make It Safe

A key element of a legalization program is a nonthreatening environment. Since the former Immigration and Naturalization Service (INS), which administered the 1986 program, has been reorganized into separate benefit and enforcement agencies, this can now be more easily achieved. Nevertheless, it is important that participants understand that the application process is free of enforcement action or threat of such action. Rapid adjudication of applications and transmittal of case decisions will also send a positive message and help assuage fears about participating in the program. Those provisions of law that would make applicants automatically deportable upon application must also be waived in legislation.

Use of community and other nongovernmental groups in the legalization program, as in 1986, would not only increase participation and the incidence of approvable applications, but would also help assure applicants that the program is safe. To the extent that there are legislative provisions to pay community groups for their assistance, provision needs to be made for prompt transfer of funds and for payment to be based on assistance provided, as well as completed applications submitted. Immigrant assistance groups in the 1986 program performed considerable work beyond the cases they submitted, which was the sole basis for their pay.

Principle 5: Promote Administrative Efficiency

Administering a legalization program is a huge task, and a new program will pose a greater challenge than the 1986 program in terms of size. Therefore, it is all the more important that the legislative design promote administrative efficiency and manageability. Experience with the 1986 program demonstrated that sufficient time to prepare for implementation is essential. While expediting the legalization process is crucial, developing the program requires time and resources. An overly short implementation schedule combined with insufficient upfront funding in 1986 resulted in incomplete and unclear administrative and operational structures, delayed regulations, insufficient outreach and public information, inadequate training, and inconsistencies in decision-making that resulted in litigation.

Fortunately, technological advances and new administrative structures and practices in place at USCIS should greatly expedite staff training and case processing, and allow the agency to handle the much larger number of legalization cases with more standardized decision-making than was possible in 1986. Nevertheless, time is required for development of standardized materials and strategies, and legislation needs to provide up-front time, funding, and expedited procurement and hiring authorities required to build additional capacity so implementation of the legalization program does not detract from the ongoing immigration and citizenship adjudicative workload. Legislation needs to provide the necessary authorities, a framework, and goals, but should leave the details of the program to the regulatory process.

Principle 6: Make All Parts of the System Work Together

Reform legislation must include complementary processes that are mutually supportive and that serve the same goals. The failure of IRCA in large part resulted from the lack of a comprehensive approach to reforming the U.S. immigration system. While attempts were made to provide legal status to many of the then-unauthorized immigrant population and prevent the unlawful entry or employment of future unauthorized immigrants, changes were not made to the legal immigration system to meet future needs in terms of either family reunification or labor demand. Furthermore, the will was lacking to end the employment of unauthorized workers, many of whom were filling jobs for which there were no other available workers.

Comprehensive immigration reform, therefore, needs to include changes to the legal immigration system that will make it more humane and more in tune with modern U.S. family-reunification, humanitarian, and labor-market needs. In doing so, legislation needs to be clear on what social-service and health benefits are available to applicants at each stage of the legalization process, recognizing that revenues from legalization and an improved legal immigration system are likely to more than offset the costs of additional access to social and health benefit programs. Reform also needs to include the means for employers to determine quickly, accurately, and definitively whether a new employee is authorized to work, and a system of enforcement that is implemented even-handedly and targeted at egregious violations that are harmful to the nation's safety and security.

6

Mass Legalization for Unauthorized Immigrants Is a Bad Idea

American Immigration Control Foundation

American Immigration Control Foundation is an immigration reform organization that aims to inform American citizens of the effects of uncontrolled immigration.

The push to grant legal status to unauthorized immigrants is about politics and money, with politicians and corporations pushing the issue, for different reasons. In reality, mass legalization will hurt the United States, is bad for US workers, exacerbates fiscal problems, fuels overpopulation and environmental degradation, and would overwhelm federal immigration workers. In addition, it will simply create the same problem down the road.

Why the big push for another mass amnesty for illegal aliens? Congress granted amnesty to nearly three million illegal aliens in 1986, and now they want to do it again.

President Barack Obama wants it, leading Democrats and Republicans in Congress want it, large corporate news media conglomerates generally support it, and so do powerful business, labor, religious, and ethnic interest groups.

The push for amnesty for the estimated 12 million or more illegal aliens living and working in the U.S. includes not just waiving the penalties for violating our immigration and labor laws. It also includes providing what supporters call "a path to citizenship" for the illegals after their penalties are waived.

It is hard for any reasonable observer to understand why a legislated amnesty should be so urgent now. After all, the economy has failed to fully recover from the downturn of 2008, which has left more than 20 million Americans unable to find full-time employment. It seems that a more sensible policy designed in the national interest would do the opposite: namely, encourage illegal immigrants to go home so that unemployed American workers wouldn't have to compete with them for scarce U.S. jobs.

It is simply not true that Americans refuse to do the work that illegal aliens do. With the exception of agriculture and very few other categories of labor, Americans are the majority of workers in all categories. As for agriculture, less than five percent of illegal aliens are farm laborers. Commonly, illegal immigrants compete with low-skilled and poverty-level Americans for jobs, while reducing the wage levels of those jobs.

Politics and Money

So why the push for amnesty? The answer is politics and money.

Hispanic voters were no more likely to support pro-immigration Republican House candidates than to support Republican candidates with records of restricting immigration.

So-called "progressive" Democrats see the transformation of illegal aliens into citizens as a new and powerful voting bloc for their party. Party strategists and activists openly admit it. Democratic political consultant Robert Creamer, a frequent visitor to the Obama White House, explicitly outlines the illegal alien strategy in his book, *Stand Up Straight: How Progressives Can Win*. He says the Democrats in Congress should grant amnesty to illegal aliens because it will enhance the party's political clout by increasing its voter base. Knowing that Hispanics vote overwhelmingly for Democrat candidates, he writes, "the immigration battle is ... important because it will have an enormous impact on the battle for power between the progressive and conservative forces in American society." He notes that the number of amnestied aliens will be added to nearly 30 million other immigrants who are already legal residents who "could apply today for citizenship, or are citizens not yet registered to vote, or immigrant voters who never go to the polls, or immigrants who will turn 18 years old this year and could register to vote." He believes that if Democrats work for issues such as amnesty that are important to immigrants, that will "define immigrants' loyalties for a generation. If we are successful, a gigantic block [sic] of progressive voters will enter the electorate over the next 15 years—a block [sic] that could be decisive in the battle for the future ..."

The Republican side of the amnesty coalition has a different motive: cheap labor. Business interests represented by the U.S. Chamber of Commerce have for many years opposed any effective enforcement of immigration laws, and have long clamored for amnesty. *The Wall Street Journal*, mouthpiece of some of the wealthiest corporations in the world, has advocated abolishing U.S. national borders altogether. In an editoral, the editors called for a constitutional amendment that would read, "There shall be open borders"!

Since the last presidential election, some Republican politicians say their party should support amnesty to attract Hispanic votes. But careful political analysts do not believe that this transparent pandering will win them a significant number of votes from a demographic that tends to oppose Republicans for many reasons other than the party's stance on immigration. As the *National Journal* noted, "on the question of big government . . . Hispanics stand most solidly with Democrats. The 2011 Pew Hispanic Center survey asked Latinos whether they would 'pay higher taxes to support a larger government or pay lower taxes and have a smaller government,' Hispanics backed higher taxes and more government by 75 percent to 19 percent."

Sen. John McCain, an outspoken amnesty supporter, won only 31 percent of the Hispanic vote in his 2008 presidential bid, the usual proportion won by other GOP [Grand Old Party, Republican] candidates. A study by political science professor George Hawley of the University of Houston found that Hispanic voters were no more likely to support pro-immigration Republican House candidates than to support Republican candidates with records of restricting immigration.

How Amnesty Hurts the United States

While amnesty and a pathway to citizenship are no doubt a benefit to the Democrat Party and the cheap labor lobby, they are a disaster for the common good. The reasons are legion.

First and foremost, amnesty and the path-to-citizenship turn the rule of law on its head. Waiving the penalty for illegal entry followed by a path-to-citizenship is a reward for law-breaking, no matter how many conditions are attached. Such reward undermines respect for law, which is a primary basis for our nation's stability and success.

Amnesty further subverts law by broadcasting to potential future illegal immigrants that the U.S. is not serious about enforcing it, that lawbreaking is ignored as long as it is widespread enough. Amnesty makes legal immigrants who have played by the rules look foolish for having complied with those rules. Amnesty followed by a path-to-citizenship also undermines the worth and significance of citizenship by granting it to people whose first act in coming here was to show contempt for Americans by breaking their laws. Governments that reward foreign lawbreakers while requiring others to hew to the law risk losing the loyalty and respect of their own citizens.

There are also many practical reasons why amnesty is a bad policy.

Amnesty Unjust for US Workers

To give amnesty to 12 million or more illegals means letting a huge number of them keep the jobs they have stolen from American workers. Federal law prohibits illegal aliens from working in the U.S. Amnesty means that they are not only forgiven for entering the country illegally, they are rewarded with keeping a job that rightfully belongs to an American worker. Right now, nearly 20 million Americans are unable to find full time employment in a sluggish economy that has not recovered from the 2008–2009 recession. It is unjust to unemployed American citizens and taxpayers to let illegal aliens keep the jobs they've illegally taken, often with stolen Social Security numbers belonging to Americans.

Center for Immigration Studies reported that 57 percent of households with children headed by a legal or illegal immigrant used at least one of eight major federal welfare programs.

Not only do aliens take jobs that rightfully belong to Americans, the unnecessary increase in the labor market drives down wages. Classic economic theory teaches that as the supply of a commodity—in this case, labor—increases, the price will fall. Increasing the labor supply simply serves to drive down wages, particularly for low-skilled jobs, which attract a large segment of the illegal alien population.

Amnesty Exacerbates US Fiscal Problems

Amnesty will add to America's fiscal crisis by vastly increasing the number of people eligible for taxpayer-funded public benefits. Because the majority of illegal aliens are uneducated and low-skilled, they are more likely when legalized to apply for taxpayer-paid benefits of some kind. Robert Rector, senior research fellow at the Heritage Foundation, discovered that "granting amnesty or legal status to illegals will generate costs in Medicare and Social Security alone of $2.5 trillion above any taxes paid in." He points out that a typical household headed by someone without a high school education pays far less in taxes than it eventually receives in benefits. He estimates it is a net cost, over time, of about $20,000 per household.

Staffers on the Senate Budget Committee found that legalizing an estimated 12 million illegal aliens will increase the costs of federally-subsidized Obamacare [Patient Protection and Affordable Care Act] health insurance anywhere from $120 billion to $200 billion in the first decade of its enactment. The Congressional Budget Office estimates that 7 million illegals are without insurance and that 85 percent of them have incomes low enough to qualify for Obamacare benefits.

Steven A. Camarota of the Center for Immigration Studies reported that 57 percent of households with children headed by a legal or illegal immigrant used at least one of eight major federal welfare programs, which include Supplemental Security Income (SSI), Temporary Assistance to Needy Families (TANF), Women, Infants and Children food program (WIC), school lunch programs, food stamps, Medicaid, and public housing and rent subsidies.

Illegal immigrants have a major impact on the cost of public education at a time when many school districts across the country are already facing significant budgetary constraints. The Center for Immigration Studies reports that school age illegal aliens and the U.S.-born children of illegal aliens are 7.2 percent—3.9 million—of the total school age population in the country. Because per-student tax expenditures in the U.S. are roughly $10,000 per year, at least $13 billion annually is required to educate illegal aliens. The U.S. Supreme Court has ruled that U.S. taxpayers must cover the costs of education for illegal alien children. If Congress grants amnesty, their parents will have no reason to take their families back to their home countries, which would relieve pressure on U.S. schools. Many schools already suffer from overcrowding, which many experts believe impairs the quality of schooling as teachers have less time to spend on each pupil. In addition, many districts flooded with illegals in states like Nevada, Arizona, Texas and California, are forced to raise taxes on citizens to pay for bilingual teachers.

Amnesty Fuels Overpopulation and Environmental Degradation

Legal status achieved by amnesty means that the estimated 12 million or more illegal aliens will be able to bring into the country family members such as spouses and children, thus contributing exponentially to America's already high population growth that is fueling overcrowding and environmental degradation.

Immigration at the current rate alone will drive U.S. population from 310 million today to a shocking 436 million by 2050, according to the U.S. Census Bureau. Immigrants and their offspring already account for more than 66 percent of the country's annual populaton growth.

That growth means dramatically increased demand for roads, schools, hospitals, fresh water and housing, all of which will have negative impacts on America's environmental capacity. Researchers say that for every person added to the U.S. population, one acre of natural habitat is lost to developed use. The amount of land area currently devoted to roads and parking lots already covers an estimated 61,000 square miles, nearly the same size as the acreage used by all U.S. farmers to plant wheat. Each year, the U.S. already paves or converts to development an area of land equal to the size of Delaware.

Whether through air pollution from the cities, increasing sprawl of suburbs, farmland conversion to development or deforestation, rapidly increasing population is undermining the natural ecological systems that facilitate our freedom and lifestyles. Overcrowding through continued massive infusions of new populations threatens to force future rationing of those natural resources and restricted consumption levels of energy and water.

Amnesty Would Overwhelm Federal Immigration Workers

The sheer size of the proposed amnesty calls into question the ability of government immigration agencies to handle the processing of so many applicants. The opportunities for fraud are rampant.

It's not as if we don't have experience with amnesty. The proposals and justifications to legalize 12 million or more illegal aliens today are precisely the same ones voiced thirty years ago when Congress considered amnesty legislation for the first time.

The congressionally approved amnesty of 1986 confirmed all of the predictions of its critics. The first was the prediction of massive fraud. Immigration authorities simply didn't have the manpower and resources to check adequately all of the 2.7 million illegal aliens who applied for the amnesty. As a result, amnesty and even citizenship were conferred on tens of thousands of illegal aliens with criminal records as overwhelmed immigration authorities were simply unable to perform the required background checks and fell victim to fraudulent document use by amnesty applicants.

The new amnesty would doubtless trigger a bureaucratic disaster, far worse than any preceding amnesty simply because of the huge numbers involved. The 1986 amnesty gave legal status to 2.7 million illegal aliens, and subsequent amnesties between 1994 and 2000 legalized about three million more. The official estimate of about 12 million illegal aliens in the U.S., is almost four times the previous mass amnesty. To appreciate the magnitude of the 12 million figure, consider that only seven of our states out of fifty have more people. Worse, a reputable study by Bear Stearns in 2005 estimated that the illegal alien population in the U.S. could be as much as 20 million!

Supporters insist it is not an amnesty, but rather "earned legalization."

In any case, the massive deluge of applications following quickly after passage of the proposed Obama amnesty would overwhelm the ability of immigration officials to screen out fraud and enforce requirements—which is not likely to be a high priority for an Obama administration anxious to increase the Democrat Party voter base.

If the government could not effectively screen out fraud with only 2.7 million applications in 1986, there is no reason to think that it could prevent significant fraud or enforce conditions with a flood of 12 million or more applications.

Even today, the Social Security Administration and the Internal Revenue Service have not cracked down on fraudulent tax forms or stolen Social Security numbers submitted by illegal aliens.

The Special Case Against the Obama Amnesty

The sponsors of the new amnesty try hard to avoid use of the word "amnesty," in order not to associate their scheme with the failed 1986 amnesty. Supporters insist it is not an amnesty, but rather "earned legalization." They point to proposed requirements that applicants pay back taxes and learn English. Former Attorney General Edwin Meese points out the fallacy of this claim by noting that the first amnesty had imposed similar conditions on applicants.

This time around some amnesty advocates claim, as they did in 1986, that increased enforcement will be part of the bargain. But the record of the 1986 amnesty and its aftermath give powerful testimony that they simply can't be trusted. The old amnesty was never followed with adequate border enforcement and sanctions on employers for hiring illegals. Nearly 30 years later, the U.S. still doesn't have a mandatory electronic system to check the legal status of employees, and there is still no system—promised long ago—to check whether people here on legal visas actually go home. The latter is most significant because at least forty percent of illegal aliens are visa overstayers, not illegal border crossers.

Amnesty advocates have already violated their promises, as Rep. Lamar Smith, R-TX has pointed out. "In fact, a compromise was agreed to back in 1986. There was a solemn vow that we would bring up amnesty one time—once, and only once—and there would be no more amnesty," he said.

The Obama administration has already demonstrated it has no intention of increasing border enforcement, and has in fact weakened border security as a matter of policy. The union representing employees of the Immigration and Customs Enforcement bureau who are responsible for border security unanimously adopted a resolution voicing "no confidence" in the agency's leadership because of its policies ordering employees to free apprehended illegals and to avoid detaining illegals who have not been convicted of felonies.

Today, the Obama administration even tries to suggest that border security is really no longer a problem. Department of Homeland Security Secretary Janet Napolitano falsely claims that the border with Mexico is already secure and under control, despite a report by the General Accountability Office (GAO) that only 129 miles of the nearly 2,000 mile Mexican border are fully secure.

We can be sure from the experience of the past 27 years that the Obama amnesty would encourage new waves of illegal immigration, just as the previous amnesty was followed by increased illegal immigration in the 1990s. It should be no surprise: rewarding an activity encourages more of it. Amnesty, if passed, will be the final declaration that our immigration laws are all for show—to be suspended on a regular basis whenever it becomes convenient for foreign law violators and selfish special interests that benefit from their presence.

Continuation of this charade is the path to anarchy, and the erosion of nationhood. Resounding defeat of the Obama amnesty is not an option for patriotic Americans; it's a necessity.

7

Yes, Amnesty Encourages More Illegal Immigration

Ian Smith

Ian Smith is an attorney in Washington, DC, and a blog contributor for the Immigration Reform Law Institute.

Two recent actions by the Barack Obama administration—Deferred Action for Childhood Arrivals (DACA) and Deferred Action for Parents of Americans (DAPA)—will incentivize more unauthorized immigrants to come to the United States, despite a recent rejection of such an argument by a Texas judge. The evidence of such incentivization is the quadrupling of unauthorized immigrants since the 1986 immigration reform and the recent surge in unaccompanied minors crossing the border without legal permission.

To the disappointment of immigration-enforcement advocates, Judge Andrew S. Hanen last week rejected a key argument that Texas raised in its attempt to establish legal standing. Texas tried to show that Obama's amnesty policies would lead to an increase of illegal aliens in the state and would strain state coffers as a consequence.

To most Americans, amnesty leading to more illegal immigration is simple cause-and-effect logic (much like "increasing the labor supply leads to lower wages"). Our court system, however, doesn't treat so-called speculative harms very well, no matter how inevitable they seem. Still, the open-borders lobby no doubt breathed a big sigh of relief at Hanen's rejection, considering the mass of evidence that Texas put forward.

Although it doesn't take a doctorate to understand that amnesty encourages illegal immigration, Texas had submitted written testimony from Harvard Ph.D. Karl Eschbach, a former demographer for the state and an expert in racial demographic trends, ethnic health disparities, and illegal immigration. With Texas paying out nearly $1.7 billion over the last two years in uncompensated health care linked to illegal aliens, the state needs this kind of expertise.

Unsurprisingly, Eschbach told the court that amnesty policies "encourage those eligible [for it] to stay in the United States and incentivize other ineligible unauthorized immigrants to remain in the United States with the hope that they will be the beneficiaries of a future adjustment of status." Further, he said, "the effect of DACA and DAPA is to incentivize residents of other countries to come to the United States."

By demonstrating that amnesty is more expensive than deportations (and far more expensive than self-deportation), we hope to confirm that the "limited resources" excuse for not enforcing our immigration laws is 100 percent false.

Judge Hanen in response noted that attorneys for Obama did "not deny that some of [the Department of Homeland Security's] action has had this effect." How *could* they have denied it? We've been experiencing "this effect" for decades. In 1986, Congress passed the Immigration Reform and Control Act providing amnesty for 3 million illegal aliens and prohibiting employers from hiring them. We ended up getting the former but not the latter. Since then, our illegal-alien population has quadrupled.

Obama's stealth amnesty in 2012 and his later promises to go "bigger and bolder" led to Texas's getting swamped with unaccompanied alien minors (UAMs) last summer. Citing the federal government's own analysis, Texas stated in its complaint that interviews with apprehended UAMs "showed overwhelmingly" that they were "motivated by the belief that they would be allowed to stay in the United States." Still, courts call this mere "speculative damage."

Strangely underutilized by Texas was UAM-surge data from Customs and Border Patrol. From 2012, when DACA was announced, to last year, UAM apprehensions increased 490 percent, 444 percent, and 610 percent for El Salvador, Guatemala, and Honduras, respectively. In the final three months of last year alone, apprehension figures for Guatemalan and El Salvadorian UAMs eclipsed their entire annual average for fiscal years 2009 through 2011—2,746 versus 1,399 for Guatemala, and 1,564 versus 1,508 for El Salvador. Even the Congressional Research Service, the *Washington Post*, and the Soros-funded Migration Policy Institute have made the link between ending the threat of deportation and the rise in illegal immigration.

Further, the federal government itself predicts an ever-bigger surge this year. Officials have stated that apprehensions for 2015 will rise to 127,000, a giant increase from the figures of recent years: 90,000 in 2014, and an average of 7,000 in 2003–11.

For taxpayers, this will be costly. From the Department of Health and Human Services—specifically, from its Office of Refugee Resettlement, just one of the agencies tasked with management of the crisis—come data showing federal grants to states and non-profit organizations rising from the already lofty $136 million in 2011 to over $800 million last year. The Immigration Law Reform Institute (which I work for) has requested, through the Freedom of Information Act, accounting records that will show the whole price tag of the amnesty-induced UAM crisis. By demonstrating that amnesty is more expensive than deportations (and far more expensive than self-deportation), we hope to confirm that the "limited re-sources" excuse for not enforcing our immigration laws is 100 percent false.

Other countries apparently understand motivating factors better than we do. Japan has one of the highest standards of living in the world and a very selective immigration system. They know that if they told the 300 million living below the poverty line in the Philippines, Indonesia, and Vietnam that they were switching to an open-borders system, Japan wouldn't be Japan for very long.

It's hoped Judge Hanen wasn't pressured by politics when deciding on this issue. The Left's increasing moralization of immigration policy is pushing out all common sense from its discussion. Given the harms of mass immigration, we need to be as right-minded as possible. Without common sense, it's the future of the country that'll become "speculative."

8

Legalization of Unauthorized Immigrants Would Benefit the US Economy

Marshall Fitz, Philip E. Wolgin, and Patrick Oakford

Marshall Fitz is director of immigration policy, Philip E. Wolgin is an immigration policy analyst, and Patrick Oakford is a research assistant at the Center for American Progress.

Despite reports to the contrary, immigrants are a net positive for the economy and pay more into the system than they take out. Legal immigrants will expand the gross domestic product (GDP) and add to the tax base. Such economic contributions will help keep Social Security solvent. Studies that purport to show that immigrants are a drain on the economy contain faulty research methods.

With immigration reform heating up in Congress and the White House putting its muscle behind legislative action, immigration opponents are already campaigning against common-sense reforms. Their current line of attack is an unsubstantiated claim that legalizing the 11 million undocumented immigrants living in the United States will be too costly for our nation. Playing to ignorant prejudice, these groups falsely suggest that immigrants are "takers"—people who use more public benefits than other groups—and that as a result, legalization would cost the United States trillions of dollars.

Mainstream economists have thoroughly debunked this general stereotype of immigrants as takers, finding that immigrants are a net positive for the economy and pay more into the system than they take out. In fact, immigrants' contributions have also played a key role in prolonging the solvency of the Social Security Trust Fund. And the truth is that the cost-benefit analyses that immigration restrictionists have used to make their wild cost projections simply are not well-rounded or accurate.

Immigrants are in fact "makers," not takers. Below, we demonstrate the clear evidence that proves this point and shoots down some of the recycled claims about the cost of immigrants to the United States.

Naturalized citizens are more economically beneficial than even legal permanent residents.

Immigrants Are a Net Positive to the Economy

Here are just a few examples of how immigrants pay more into the U.S. economy than they take out.

Large GDP [gross domestic product] gains and tax revenue from legalization

Research by UCLA [University of California, Los Angeles] Professor Raúl Hinojosa-Ojeda shows that legalizing our nation's undocumented immigrant population and reforming our legal immigration system would add a cumulative $1.5 trillion to U.S. GDP over a decade. These big gains occur because legalized workers earn higher wages than undocumented workers, and they use those wages to buy things such as houses, cars, phones, and clothing. As more money flows through the U.S. economy, businesses grow to meet the demand for more goods and services, and more jobs and economic value are created. Hinojosa-Ojeda found that the tax benefits alone from legalization would be between $4.5 billion and $5.4 billion in the first three years.

Big economic boost from the DREAM [Development, Relief, and Education for Alien Minors] Act

Research by [University of] Notre Dame economists Juan Carlos Guzmán and Raúl Jara finds that passing the DREAM Act would add $329 billion to the U.S. economy by 2030. The DREAM Act provides a double boost to the economy: First, DREAMers will be able to work legally (generally at higher wages), and second, because of the requirements to complete high school and some college or military service, they will have more education and training, which translates into better and higher-paying jobs. All of these extra wages circulate through the economy, supporting new job creation for the native born as well.

Naturalized citizens earn even more

A large body of literature illustrates that naturalized citizens are more economically beneficial than even legal permanent residents. In the United States the University of Southern California's Manuel Pastor estimated that naturalized citizens earn between 8 percent and 11 percent higher wages after naturalization. Pastor concludes that if even half of those who are currently eligible—the Department of Homeland Security estimates that there are more than 8.5 million people in this category—became citizens, it would add between $21 billion and $45 billion to the U.S. economy over five years.

Even undocumented immigrants pay taxes

Immigrants—even the undocumented—pay a significant amount of money in taxes each year. A 2011 study by the Institute for Taxation and Economic Policy found that undocumented immigrants paid $11.2 billion in state and local taxes in 2010 alone, adding a significant amount of money to help state and local finances. It is important to note that immigrants—even legal immigrants—are barred from most social services, meaning that they pay to support benefits they cannot receive.

Immigrants help keep Social Security solvent

According to the National Foundation for American Policy, immigrants will add a net of $611 billion to the Social Security system over the next 75 years. Immigrants are a key driver of keeping the Social Security Trust Fund solvent, and Stuart Anderson of the National Foundation for American Policy finds that cutting off immigration to the country would increase the size of the Social Security deficit by 31 percent over 50 years.

Snapshot Accounting Leads to Faulty Conclusions

Even with these positive economic benefits, though, anti-immigrant groups continue to insist that immigrants take more out of the system than they pay into it. Two studies in particular have received attention lately: a 2007 study by the Heritage Foundation, which found that legalization would cost $2.6 trillion; and a 2011 study by the Center for Immigration Studies, which concluded that Hispanic immigrants use more public benefits than other groups.

Both studies rely on a snapshot of immigrants frozen in time to get to their calculations. Heritage focuses only on immigrants as retirees without taking into account the money they pay into the system during their working years. The Center for Immigration Studies focuses on families with children without taking into account the taxes their children will pay over their lifetime. Each approach is predicated on faulty assumptions.

Heritage Foundation study: A misleading snapshot of immigrant life

In an attention-grabbing headline from 2007, the Heritage Foundation's Robert Rector argued that legalizing undocumented immigrants would cost taxpayers "at least $2.6 trillion." The message was deceptively simple: At some point in the future, the legalized immigrants will hit age 67 and will retire. Once retired, these immigrants will cost taxpayers a significant amount of money by using programs such as Social Security and Medicare—a figure the author estimated to be roughly $17,000 per year for an average of 18 years. Multiply the ensuing $306,000 by the 8.5 million legalized adults whom Rector expects to reach retirement age, and that's how you get $2.6 trillion.

The missing context: Immigrants pay into the system long before retiring

The problem with such magical thinking is that Rector failed to provide basic context for his conclusions: Most importantly, he only looks at the costs of immigrants once they retire and does not take into account any taxes they would have paid into the system as workers preretirement. All retirees use more in services than they contribute in taxes during retirement years, but the explicit bargain of programs such as Social Security is that you pay into the system over your lifetime and then take from it once you retire.

Immigrants receive less in Social Security and Medicare benefits than their descendants in the second generation and the native-born population.

In addition to the fact that the study only considers a portion of the lifetime contributions—those made during retirement—of immigrants, Rector incorrectly assesses the fiscal cost of immigrants during retirement by, for example, assuming that all undocumented immigrants lack a high school education. Even if such an outlandish claim were true—and according to the Pew Hispanic Center, only 49 percent of undocumented immigrants lack a high school degree—it is almost certain that a portion of the immigrant community would gain more education after legalization, leading to higher wages and thus higher tax contributions to Social Security and Medicare.

Rector also claims that immigrant retirees will impose a net cost of $17,000 per year, but provides no explanation or citation for how he came to this estimate. Without knowing how he came up with that figure, it is impossible to know if that is even the correct annual net fiscal impact of immigrant retirees, let alone if it is offset by payments into the system over the working life of the immigrants.

The bottom line: Immigrants receive less in Social Security than the native born

Finally, the Heritage study fails to acknowledge that research shows that immigrant retirees are less likely to use the benefits than native-citizen retirees. Demographers James P. Smith and Barry Edmonston, for example, found that immigrants receive less in Social Security and Medicare benefits than their descendants in the second generation and the native-born population. And an analysis of the 2012 March Current Population Survey data also indicates that immigrants who receive Social Security get less in benefits than native-born recipients. To insinuate that immigrant retirees will be an added burden to the American taxpayer is therefore simply false.

Center for Immigration Studies report: Erroneous comparisons hide the fact that immigrants are no more likely to use social services than the native born

The Center for Immigration Studies released a report in 2011 concluding that "57 percent of households headed by an immigrant (legal and illegal) with children (under 18) used at least one welfare program, compared to 39 percent for native households with children." The report attempted to paint immigrants—and Hispanic immigrants in particular—as a burden on U.S. social services. This could not be further from the truth.

The study reaches these conclusions by manipulating the data analysis. The study relied on, for example, an unconventionally broad definition of welfare, which included programs for children such as free and reduced-price school lunches. No other comparable study on welfare usage includes such programs in their calculations.

Comparing apples to oranges: Report fails to control for income level and household composition

The Center for Immigration Studies also obfuscates its findings by using a faulty unit for comparison. Instead of comparing all household users of welfare benefits, it limits its analysis to families with children. This arbitrary data restriction eliminates the possibility of accurately comparing—at the household level—welfare-participation rates between immigrants and natives. If you are going to compare households, you must compare *all* households.

But most troublesome is the fact that the Center for Immigration Studies compares immigrant and native-born welfare rates without controlling for differences in income levels. Comparing welfare-participation rates without accounting for differences in income level is akin to comparing the welfare-participation rates of a highly developed country to that of an underdeveloped country—it is clear that an underdeveloped country would have a greater number of welfare users.

If one controls for income level and considers all households, the story of immigrants being a drain on social programs disappears.

The bottom line: No difference in welfare usage among the native and foreign born

Demographers Randy Capps, Michael Fix, and Everett Henderson, for example, compared welfare-participation rates of legal permanent resident immigrants to the native born. When controlling for income, they found that immigrants had similar—if not lower—participation rates than natives in the three main social programs: welfare, food stamps, and Medicaid. At the 200 percent poverty line—a common threshold for low-income households—32 percent of native families received food stamps, compared to 22 percent of naturalized-citizen immigrant families.

An analysis of the 2012 March Current Population Survey data that controls for income and includes all households reveals that the results of [Jeffrey] Passel and Fix's [Urban Institute] study still hold true today—immigrants use social programs such as Medicaid and Supplemental Security Income at similar rates to native households.

Over the next few weeks [early 2013], the House and Senate will hold hearings on immigration reform, and no doubt anti-immigrant groups will increasingly characterize immigrants as "takers." Americans should not be fooled, though.

The facts are clear: Immigrants are not a drain on the U.S. economy. Immigrants are no more dependent on welfare programs than the native born. Legalization would not cost U.S. taxpayers trillions of dollars. The only thing the United States can't afford is to have the efforts of Congress and the president derailed by anti-immigrant groups that are dedicated to hiding the truth: Immigrants are makers, not takers.

9

Legalization of Unauthorized Immigrants Would Burden the US Economy

Federation for American Immigration Reform

Federation for American Immigration Reform (FAIR) is a non-profit organization that supports border security and lower immigration levels.

The February 2013 argument by the Center for American Progress—which claims that the legalization of unauthorized immigrants would benefit the economy—is flawed. The research cited in support of this rosy conclusion does not actually show that workers legalized under the 1986 Immigration Reform and Control Act had wage gains from the change in legal status. In fact, there is reason to believe that the group legalized under the 1986 reform has become more of a fiscal burden on the United States.

The left-wing Center for American Progress (CAP) recently released [February 2013] a polemic arguing that a general amnesty should again be adopted—like the one in 1986—because it would be a boost to the U.S. economy. This campaign is an effort to counter the findings by FAIR [Federation for American Immigration Reform], the Center for Immigration Studies and the Heritage Foundation that the amnesty proposal would have a profound negative budgetary impact. CAP relied on flawed analysis to justify its conclusion that an amnesty would benefit the economy. It treated illegal alien residents as if they were the same as legal immigrants and a benefit to the economy. This deliberate conflation of illegal aliens and legal immigrants is designed to support CAP's political goal of enacting another amnesty in 2013.

A Rosy Conclusion

Illegal aliens have a very different economic profile than legal immigrants. The act of making illegal aliens into legal residents by an amnesty does not change their human capital and suddenly make them greater contributors to the economy the same as immigrants sponsored by an employer. While all workers contribute to the Gross Domestic Product, that is not the same as saying that low-wage workers contribute as much as middle or high-wage workers or that they are not a fiscal burden on the U.S. taxpayer.

One of the studies cited by the CAP report in support of its misleading assertion, was research by UCLA [University of California, Los Angeles] Professor Raúl Hinojosa-Ojeda published by CAP in 2010. Hinojosa argued that, "The historical experience of legalization under the 1986 Immigration Reform and Control Act, or IRCA indicates that comprehensive immigration reform would raise wages, increase consumption, create jobs, and generate additional tax revenue." The problem with that assessment of the IRCA amnesty is that it is counterfactual.

To support his rosy conclusion, Hinojosa cited a survey of the legalized IRCA beneficiaries done five years after the amnesty. But, he either did not understand the findings of that survey report or chose to mischaracterize them. The survey report did find that real wages for the amnesty recipients had increased, but they had not increased any more than they had for comparable U.S. workers (non-supervisory, non-farm, wage earners). Both groups experienced wage increases of 15 percent over the period. Therefore, it was the change in the general economy that produced wage gains, not the amnesty. Similarly, the survey found that the earnings gap between amnesty recipients and other wage earners continued to exist despite the intervening five years of legal status for the former illegal aliens.

By 1992, the likelihood of unemployment was higher for legalized than for other U.S. men—a reversal of the pattern seen prior to legalization.

Even more significant, the 1996 study found that there was a significant difference between the amnesty recipients who were visa overstayers—mostly foreign students—and those who entered without authorization. The former were better educated and were more likely to speak English well. These overstayers did experience some earnings benefit from the amnesty relative to other workers. However, the fact that this group gained while overall the amnesty beneficiaries did not gain, means that the non-overstayers lost ground economically over the five-year period following the amnesty. A possible explanation for that lost ground was the surge in new illegal immigration touched off by the adoption of the amnesty that created greater job competition for low-wage workers.

The Truth About Past Amnesty Recipients

An even more troubling conclusion from the 1996 survey is that its findings related to an unrepresentative sample of the 1986 amnesty beneficiaries. Though not the fault of the administrators of the survey, it did not include data collected from the two-fifths of the amnesty recipients who gained legal status as a result of their working in the agriculture sector. It is reasonable to assume that the profile of those who entered the country illegally and were included in the survey was also representative of those who applied for amnesty as agricultural workers—though one could make the argument that agricultural workers as a group had even less education and work skills.

Accordingly, it is also reasonable to assume that the bulk of the amnesty recipients—combining the two-fifths not in the survey with those in the survey who had similar characteristics—lost ground economically when compared to others in the workforce. Recognition of this phenomenon is particularly relevant to the current amnesty discussion, because any new legislation is likely to again include special provisions for illegal aliens who have worked in agriculture.

Hinojosa would not have had to look far in the survey report to find evidence that it did not justify his rosy assessment. The following are quotes from the 1996 survey report:

".. by 1992, the likelihood of unemployment was higher for legalized than for other U.S. men—a reversal of the pattern seen prior to legalization."

"Legal status, employment, and long hours of work notwithstanding, many of those admitted under section 245A have had difficulty keeping their families out of poverty."

"Receiving only a grade school education in a non-English-speaking country is likely to afford the entrant little mobility in the U.S. labor market. IRCA-mandated English language classes have not altered this situation. In 1992, nearly one-quarter of all legalized adults still reported that they spoke no English."

".. data show that the sufficiently skilled were often able to find better jobs without work authorization, while the most unskilled could not do so even with appropriate documents."

".. in 1991, 34 percent of legalization families, as compared with 17 percent of families nationwide, lived on annual incomes of less than $15,000."

"Thus in 1992, after 5 years of legal U.S. residence, a disproportionate share of legalization families were still below the poverty threshold."

The data on the amnesty recipients five years after legal-ization clearly suggest a conclusion diametrically opposed to the characterization given to those findings by Hinojosa: Most beneficiaries of the 1986 amnesty had not become greater eco-nomic contributors as a result of the amnesty. Rather, their marginal participation in the economy meant that when they became eligible to draw on social service programs available to them after five years as legal residents, they became much more of a fiscal burden on the U.S. taxpayer at the federal, state and local level.

10

The Green Economy and a Path to Citizenship

David Foster

David Foster is the founding executive director of the BlueGreen Alliance, a national partnership of labor unions and environmental organizations.

Many immigrants today are environmental refugees, driven to migrate by climate change and other environmental issues. Unauthorized immigrants suffer more from severe weather associated with climate change, unable to obtain federal relief. In addition, unauthorized immigrants are disproportionately exposed to environmental hazards. Environmentalists should support immigration reform that includes a path to citizenship, as it is both morally required and could increase support for climate action.

President Teddy Roosevelt's assertion that "far and away the best prize that life offers is the chance to work hard at work worth doing" rings as true today as it did a century ago. While that pursuit is something that unites us all, in today's world many people never have a chance to work, much less to have "work worth doing." For more than 200 years, our immigrant nation and our American Dream have inspired the world to believe that both were possible. And it's why today, as environmentalists, we need to support an equitable path to citizenship.

The rise of immigration is not solely a US phenomenon. Globally, immigration between countries and within countries has increased dramatically as a result of a variety of factors. However, two important ones are economic desperation and climate-related disasters. The two are mutually reinforcing. As far back as 1990, the Intergovernmental Panel on Climate Change forecast that the greatest effect of climate change on human society would be forced migration. In the mid-1990s the International Red Cross estimated that there were already 25 million environmental refugees. Today the IPCC estimates there will be as many as 200 million climate refugees by 2050.

In the case of the US, droughts in sub-Saharan Africa and the resulting conflicts over land and water brought thousands of Somalis to Maine and Minnesota. In the 1990s, monocrop agriculture pushed by US agribusiness drove Mexican and Central American farmers off their land, leading to a north-ward exodus to the US. While the causes are always complex and multifaceted, climate change is an amplifying factor. For the environmental movement to turn a blind eye to those whose lives have been uprooted by climate change would be both tragic and a missed opportunity to change the politics of climate change.

Almost everyone would agree that America's immigration system is broken. Approximately 11 million people live in the US without the rights citizenship affords. The hope of a job with better opportunities is what brings people to leave everything they know for a new life—"the chance to work hard at work worth doing."

The reality is that our economy needs immigrants.

But the system as it exists too often allows unscrupulous employers to violate minimum wage and overtime laws, and to force undocumented immigrants to work in dangerous working conditions. Every year, thousands of undocumented immigrants are injured or killed on the job due to unsafe working conditions. In contrast, those with citizenship and union members whose working conditions are protected are less likely to suffer injury on the job.

In addition, undocumented immigrant communities are more likely than other populations to bear the brunt of the effects of severe weather associated with climate change. Take, for example, two of the most destructive hurricanes in recent memory—Hurricane Katrina and Hurricane Sandy. While non-citizens are eligible for disaster relief if they have the proper documentation and verification, undocumented immigrants affected by Hurricane Sandy were left out of federal relief efforts. The Mexican Consulate in Manhattan has estimated that at least 380 of its citizens in New York and New Jersey suffered losses because of Sandy. Without insurance and without a Social Security number, immigrants suffer in silence, rebuilding on their own rather than risking deportation. The environmental movement has a responsibility to give voice to those who bear the heaviest load of severe climate events.

Beyond severe weather disasters, undocumented immigrants are also disproportionately exposed to environmental hazards where they live and work. Farmworkers, most of whom are undocumented, are routinely exposed to toxic pesticides on fruits and vegetables. A 2007 study of the San Francisco Bay Area found that immigrants are nearly twice as likely to live within one mile of a pollution facility.

It would be an oversight to debate immigration reform without acknowledging the contributions of immigrant communities. The reality is that our economy needs immigrants. Our nation's competitiveness has historically relied on the hard work and rich perspectives of immigrants. America's factories, cities, and scientific know-how have benefited from their contributions. Where would we be without, for example, Albert Einstein who was granted citizenship in 1940, or lesser known inventor Elihu Thompson, who is credited in part with the formation of General Electric? Immigrants are 40 percent more likely to start businesses than native-born Americans.

Some environmental opponents of immigration reform believe that encouraging immigration reinforces overconsumption of resources and energy in the US. But restricting immigration simply tries to check environmental problems at the border. Disenfranchising those who, in many cases, are climate refugees is indefensible. As the effects of increasingly severe weather events unfold, who can be in favor of denying the core human rights of up to 200 million climate refugees?

In the US, this disenfranchisement alienates a key constituency—the broader immigrant community—from supporting comprehensive climate action. Polling shows that some of the strongest support for environmental reform is among immigrant communities. Standing up for an equitable path to citizenship for our country's 11 million undocumented workers is morally right and, politically, an essential part of the strategy to win comprehensive climate legislation.

Immigration reform itself is "work worth doing." I would challenge my environmental colleagues to join with me in pushing for an equitable path to citizenship.

11

A Path to Citizenship Should Not Be a Part of Immigration Reform

Peter Skerry

Peter Skerry is a political science professor at Boston College and a fellow of the Brookings Institution.

There is a compromise on immigration reform between deportation and full legalization with a path to citizenship: permanent noncitizen resident status. This mere legalization would allow unauthorized immigrants to have a legal status but would never allow them to become citizens. This third way is attractive as it makes both the United States and unauthorized immigrants take responsibility for the current state of immigration in the country.

The debate over U.S. immigration policy has been rebooted. There now appears to be bipartisan support for what's generally called comprehensive reform. But a stumbling block remains: What to do about the estimated 11 million illegal immigrants among us. Deportation? Complete amnesty? A "path" to citizenship?

Permanent Noncitizen Residency

There is a way forward, and it can be best summarized by "none of the above." It lies, instead, between these choices. It's legalization without citizenship.

Peter Skerry, "A Third Way on Immigration," *Los Angeles Times*, December 16, 2012.

With as few conditions and as broadly as possible, we should offer undocumented immigrants status as "permanent noncitizen residents." Unlike current green card holders, these individuals would never have the option of naturalizing and becoming U.S. citizens. The only exception would be for minors who arrived here with their parents. Provided they have not committed any serious crimes, such individuals should be immediately eligible for citizenship.

Simplicity is one distinct virtue of this approach. The prospect of mass deportations (or the hope of mass self-deportations) is both unpalatable and impractical. And establishing and implementing a complicated pathway to citizenship—or even to a lesser legal status—requires more faith than most Americans have in our government's ability to administer programs effectively and fairly.

For example, one proposal has called for the undocumented to return to their native countries for some period of time and then apply for a visa and "get in line" to return to the U.S. legally. But how would the return trip be monitored? And after that, how effectively would the visa quotas and readmission processes be administered? What would happen when an aging grandmother is returned to a "home" she left 30 years ago, or when illegal parents and their U.S.-born teenagers find themselves on different sides of the divide?

A Compromise of Mere Legalization

Most Americans understand that undocumented immigrants came here primarily because there were jobs waiting for them, and that American employers and consumers have benefited from their labor. They find it difficult to avoid the conclusion that all Americans are complicit in this problem.

Yet in an era of increasing inequality, others insist they do not see themselves benefiting from the presence of illegals, or of unskilled immigrants generally. And while economic studies consistently demonstrate that there is substantially less competition with immigrants for jobs than many believe, opponents of immigration, especially of illegal immigration, are not wrong when they point to negative impacts on the quality of life in their neighborhoods and to the fiscal burdens on their schools, hospitals and other social service providers.

> *The overwhelming majority of those [immigrants] covered by [former President Ronald] Reagan's amnesty have settled for less than full citizenship.*

My proposal—let's call it "mere legalization"—speaks directly to these Americans. To be sure, it would not treat undocumented immigrants as criminals, as many insist. But neither would it treat them as mere victims. It would, as President [Barack] Obama put it at American University in 2010, "demand responsibility from people living here illegally." Those who chose as adults to take enormous risks and break our laws would be held accountable as responsible agents who must now pay a clear and enduring penalty. Looking forward, any such initiative would have to be accompanied by rigorous and comprehensive enforcement efforts not only along our borders and ports of entry but at work sites throughout the land.

Immigrant advocates and their supporters may reject mere legalization as too punitive, as "second-class citizenship." Yet a quarter of a century after President [Ronald] Reagan's amnesty went into effect in 1987, only two-fifths of those who became legal permanent residents through that program have gone on to become citizens. In light of restrictions imposed in the 1990s on noncitizen eligibility for various federal social welfare benefits, and subsequent programs to increase naturalization rates, such low numbers are particularly striking. Traditionally low levels of naturalization among eligible Mexican-origin immigrants are one factor at work here. Yet the point remains: The overwhelming majority of those covered by

Reagan's amnesty have settled for less than full citizenship. So what exactly are we arguing about?

A Practical, Achievable Policy

To those who think that permanent noncitizen status is too lenient, I would respond that much would depend on the specifics of any such program, about which Congress would have enormous latitude to do as it sees fit. Even so, under current law and policy, green card holders are treated differently from citizens. Besides not being eligible for certain government jobs and social programs, they are not permitted to serve on state or federal juries. And of course noncitizens do not vote in federal and state elections, though they may in a few local jurisdictions.

When green card holders travel outside the U.S., especially for extended periods, they currently risk being not allowed to reenter. As UCLA [University of California, Los Angeles] law professor Hiroshi Motomura concludes, under prevailing rulings "the Constitution protects a returning lawful immigrant no more than a first-time entrant."

More generally, noncitizen residents have no absolute assurance that they will be allowed to remain here. Failing to keep documents current or committing various crimes, including tax evasion and shoplifting, could result in their deportation. So the status of green card holders is highly contingent on their own behavior and on global politics. And unlike U.S. citizens, they cannot obtain visas for immediate family members outside the usual numerical quotas.

The underlying point is easily lost in the fog of rancorous debate over punishment or amnesty for the 11 million undocumented immigrants among us: The United States is a remarkably absorptive and open society, where newcomers and their children put down roots and develop ties very quickly. Indeed, our openness is so powerful that many among the undocumented have been noisily demanding relief. Why not allow ourselves to feel good about this and use it to propel us toward a middle path?

We don't have to choose between granting citizenship to lawbreakers or imposing onerous penalties that we lack the will and means to implement and enforce. We can choose instead a practical, achievable policy that acknowledges Americans' share of responsibility for this mess, but that also requires illegal immigrants to acknowledge theirs.

12

Should There Be a Path to Citizenship?

Mark Krikorian

Mark Krikorian is executive director of the Center for Immigration Studies and author of The New Case Against Immigration: Both Legal and Illegal.

There are many arguments put forth in favor of granting unauthorized immigrants legal status without a path to citizenship. Some support it because the 1986 immigration reform—which did grant a path to citizenship—was such a failure. For others the denial of an option of citizenship is a punishment for breaking the law. Many see it as a compromise that avoids some of the pitfalls of full citizenship such as sponsoring other family members and voting. Nonetheless, such a compromise should be avoided because it would create a two-tier society.

Congress will face many questions when it takes on immigration this year [2013]: Should illegal immigrants be given legal status? Should we raise or lower the number of new immigrants? Should we shift toward taking more skilled workers and fewer relatives of earlier immigrants?

But there's another question that has bedeviled our immigration policy for hundreds of years: Should newcomers, or illegal immigrants receiving amnesty, be put on a path to citizenship or be given a status that would permit them to legally work and travel but wouldn't culminate in citizenship?

This is shaping up as a dividing line between the major political parties. Republican Sen. Marco Rubio of Florida made waves last year by suggesting an amnesty for young illegal immigrants who came here as children (one of the many spin-offs of the Dream Act), but giving them work visas rather than citizenship. Something along these lines was introduced late last year in the form of the Achieve Act by retiring Republican Sens. Jon Kyl of Arizona and Kay Bailey Hutchison of Texas. Even the conservative policy journal *National Affairs* has an article by a respected political scientist making the case for such an approach for the bulk of the illegal immigrant population.

Democrats generally have pressed for a path to full citizenship for illegal immigrants and for future foreign workers. As far back as 1885, the embryonic labor movement helped pass the Alien Contract Labor Law, which prohibited the importation of guest workers. More recently, the issue caused dissension within the labor movement during the 2006–07 round of immigration debates. The Service Employees International Union made a strategic decision to ally with the U.S. Chamber of Commerce in supporting a large guest worker program as the price of passing a "comprehensive" immigration reform bill. The AFL-CIO [American Federation of Labor and Congress of Industrial Organizations], on the other hand, stayed true to its opposition to contract labor, as did a number of Senate Democrats, including Barack Obama.

Politicians on the left and the right are constantly trying to weasel out of the word "amnesty," even though that's the word for legalizing illegal immigrants.

A number of arguments are offered for the non-citizenship approach:

First—and this is more a sentiment than an argument—the previous big amnesty gave full immigrant status to illegal immigrants, and it was a colossal failure. The Immigration Reform and Control Act of 1986 didn't fail because of the kind of status offered, of course (it failed because promises to enforce the law in the future were ignored), but it rightly leaves a bad taste in the mouth. More practically, as Boston College Professor Peter Skerry points out in the aforementioned *National Affairs* article, by 2009, fully two decades after getting their green cards, only about 41 percent of the 2.7 million illegal immigrants who benefited from the 1986 law had become naturalized citizens.

Some claim that giving illegal immigrants work visas rather than citizenship is an appropriate punishment, given that they knew what they were doing when they settled here illegally, and subsequently broke a whole series of other laws—tax fraud, identity theft, etc. Skerry calls it "a clear and decisive penalty." This has some merit, because the other penalties that illegal immigrants would be subject to under various reform proposals—notably large fines—are merely for public consumption. Few illegal immigrants could afford $10,000 per person to become legal residents, and so the fines would certainly be waived, resulting in no real penalty at all.

Another appeal of the non-citizenship option is that it somehow would not represent amnesty. Politicians on the left and the right are constantly trying to weasel out of the word "amnesty," even though that's the word for legalizing illegal immigrants. But focus-group research told amnesty supporters that the word was to be avoided and, ever since, they've insisted that some feature or other makes their latest proposal "not amnesty."

Visa holders would also not be able to sponsor future immigrants. That means both that such an amnesty wouldn't spark a significant wave of additional immigration down the road and also that the relatives of today's illegal immigrants would not be rewarded with citizenship themselves.

Finally, giving illegal immigrants or foreign workers a status short of citizenship keeps them from voting. This isn't as clear an indictment of Republican supporters of this approach as it may seem; Democrats from Barney Frank to SEIU [Service Employees International Union] President Eliseo Medina have been explicit in promoting mass immigration for nakedly political purposes, so it's no surprise that their opponents should also consider its political impact.

My own view is that we should admit fewer foreign workers, not more, and that amnesty is appropriate at this time only for illegal immigrants who've lived here since they were infants or toddlers. But whomever we do admit, or give amnesty to, should be given a path to full membership in our society. The alternative moves us toward the kind of two-tiered society we see in Saudi Arabia, a model we should do our best to avoid.

13

Immigration Reform as a Path to Conscience, Not Just Citizenship

Christian Science Monitor

The Christian Science Monitor *is an independent international news organization.*

One of the central puzzles in the immigration debate is how to grant legal status to people who have broken the law without undermining the rule of law. Deporting unauthorized immigrants is impractical and allowing them to stay living in the shadows is unreasonable. There must be a punishment that fits the crime and deters recurrence, with the sole purpose of improving compliance with US immigration law. The right consequences will help improve respect for immigration laws that have gone unenforced for too long.

How much are Americans willing to forgive the 11 million people now living in the United States illegally?

Answer that and you might be able to predict what Congress will do in its latest drive to solve the immigration puzzle.

A bipartisan group of senators has agreed on the outlines for immigration reforms, one of which would grant current illegal immigrants a path to legal status under "tough but fair" conditions. And President Obama is pitching his own reforms.

At the heart of this political struggle is the issue of forgiving illegal immigrants for breaking US law, either by illegal border crossings or overstaying visas. Many in Congress now accept that it would be impractical and potentially immoral to deport so many people. And keeping such immigrants estranged in society only keeps them dangerously underground.

Yet any forgiveness often comes with terms attached, such as limited penalties for tax evaders in a government amnesty. What kind of punishment would fit an admitted crime but also deter its recurrence?

The terms of forgiveness on a mass scale are meant not only to help offenders become honest and law-abiding residents but also help restore the consensus that rules are worth following. Enforcement of any laws can only go so far. Society also needs shared values—such as a desire for secure borders—along with having a majority of residents who will feel the pangs of conscience if they break the law.

That's why the Internal Revenue Service is more lenient to those who volunteer a tax violation than those who are caught. There's an underlying assumption that people not only want to obey the law and avoid punishment but also want to pay taxes as a matter of societal goodwill.

Many Americans who oppose legal status for illegal immigrants fear an erosion of this consensus about rule of law. A conditional amnesty now might provide an incentive for more people to enter the US in expectation of a future amnesty. Case in point: A 1986 amnesty for an estimated 4 million illegals at the time helped attract many of today's illegal immigrants.

To reduce this fear, the group of senators laid out a number of legal and security hoops before full legalization is granted. A special commission will monitor progress in securing borders. Employers will need to verify they have hired only legal workers. To earn provisional status, illegal immigrants will need to register, pay a fine and back taxes, and pass a background check.

Ultimately earning citizenship will take even more steps, such as going to the back of the line of prospective immigrants who have already applied legally.

The purpose of these kinds of stiff requirements should be to improve compliance with immigration law, not undercut it. Finding the right balance must not be a political exercise that caters to pressure groups. It should be based on restoring the nation's conscience about immigration laws after years of lax enforcement—caused in part by a widespread desire for cheap labor and a willingness to look the other way.

The many examples of tax amnesties by states provide a lesson. Many of those amnesties failed to achieve a long-term increase in tax compliance because they were not coupled with strong and sustained enforcement.

Merely promising better immigration enforcement is not enough. Results must be measurable and for years. And legalization, or even amnesty, must be seen as a tool to restore respect for immigration laws.

If illegal immigrants admit they broke the law and suffer some consequences, then they, too, will be displaying the sort of individual conscience that is the most critical element in enforcement of law—honesty and consideration toward others in society.

14

A Guest-Worker Program Is the Best Immigration Reform

Ben Carson

Pediatric neurosurgeon Ben Carson is an emeritus professor at the Johns Hopkins School of Medicine and a candidate for the Republican nomination for president in 2016. He is also the author of One Nation: What We Can All Do to Save America's Future.

There is a need for immigration reform legislation in the United States to fix the broken immigration system. Currently, the borders are unsecured and incentives make it easy for unauthorized immigrants to stay and work. Rather than granting legal status to those here illegally, a guest-worker program should be enacted that requires individuals to leave and apply from outside the country. In addition, laws against hiring unauthorized workers must be enforced, the borders must be secured, and those that break the law must be deported.

We have all heard it said many times that America is a land of immigrants, some voluntary and some involuntary, but immigrants nevertheless.

The Need for Legislation

We have plenty of space in our country, but insufficient resources to support everyone who wants to come here. When we see innocent children used as political pawns, it still tugs at our heartstrings, which is the desired intent. The real question is, what are we going to do about it?

Immigration reform has been a very tough issue, as well as a political football, and it has produced governmental stalemates and no useful solutions for decades. President [Barack] Obama's decision to act unilaterally outside of Congress is not the answer.

Instead, Congress must use its lawmaking powers to fix a system that is so broken that only a legislative solution can fix it. The lack of policy progress has been incredibly frustrating, and the humanitarian border crisis this summer [2014] only highlighted how badly we need a system that deals efficiently and effectively with both illegal and legal immigration.

It is time for Congress to act and to do so in a bipartisan fashion that engenders the confidence of the American people. There are many common-sense prescriptions within reach of our government. It is time to seize them.

The Issues to Be Addressed

To begin to solve this problem, we must first have some understanding of why it exists. Despite all of its problems, America is still the place of dreams. As such, it is small wonder that so many from other nations would like to live here.

A national guest-worker program makes sense and seems to work well in Canada.

Right now, we have very porous borders and unenthusiastic and inconsistent enforcement of immigration laws. Further incentives for illegal immigration are easy enrollment in public schools, easy employment for those willing to take jobs others don't want, easy access to healthcare and easy acquisition of public support through welfare programs. Yet this population cannot participate in the formal workforce, which means they cannot contribute fully to their local economies.

Any discussion of immigration reform should include bipartisan solutions that both address the undocumented population here today and discourage illegal immigration going forward. If these issues are not addressed, solutions will fall short.

On the other hand, if all of these issues are addressed firmly and consistently, we can uphold the rule of law and discourage further illegal immigration. Detractors will say that if it were that simple, it already would have been done and we wouldn't be having this discussion. What they fail to account for is the fact that the issues have not been addressed. A national guest-worker program makes sense and seems to work well in Canada.

A Guest-Worker Program

Noncitizens would have to apply for a guest-worker permit and have a guaranteed job awaiting them. Taxes would be paid at a rate commensurate with other U.S. workers, and special visas would allow for easy entry and egress across borders. Guest-worker status would be granted to individuals and not to groups.

People already here illegally could apply for guest-worker status from outside of the country. This means they would have to leave first. They should in no way be rewarded for having broken our laws, but if they are wise, they will arrange with their employer before they leave to immediately offer them a legal job as soon as their application is received.

When they return, they still would not be U.S. citizens, but they would be legal, and they would be paying taxes. Only jobs that are vacant as a result of a lack of interest by American citizens should be eligible for the guest-worker program. In return for greater certainty on immigration, employers must bear some responsibility for making sure that no illegal immigrants are hired.

Employers who break the rules should receive swift, severe, and consistent punishment that constitutes a real deterrent and not a mere inconvenience. A second infraction should be a criminal offense and treated as such.

Upholding the Rule of Law

All of this is irrelevant unless we have secure borders. There is much that can be learned from security personnel in prisons and other secured facilities, and there is a great deal of smart technology that can be employed to achieve secure borders. It is a matter of will rather than ability.

As long as we reward people who break laws, they will continue to break laws. We do need a continual flow of immigrants, but choosers need not be beggars. We make decisions based on our needs. People who refuse to comply with the rules must forfeit chances of legalization in the future.

Anyone caught involved in voter fraud should be immediately deported and have his citizenship revoked. The point is this: We must create a system that disincentivizes illegal immigration and upholds the rule of law while providing us with a steady stream of immigrants from other nations who will strengthen our society. Let's solve the problem and stop playing political football.

15

Amnesty Is the Only Feasible Solution to the Immigration Problem

Ed Krayewski

Ed Krayewski is an associate editor at Reason.com.

The term "amnesty" has become a pejorative, with supporters of immigration reform that includes a path to citizenship denying it constitutes amnesty and opponents labeling it as such in an attempt to discredit the proposal. But actually such reform is a kind of amnesty and it is the only feasible solution to the immigration problem. It ought to be supported because immigration is good for the economy and a natural right; unauthorized immigrants already pay taxes and are otherwise law-abiding; and there are too many unauthorized immigrants to do anything else.

Immigration reform returned to center stage in Washington last week [January 29, 2013] with a proposal from a bipartisan group of senators that was promptly endorsed in principle by President Barack Obama. One of the lynchpins of the proposal is providing a "path to citizenship" for those who are currently in the country illegally, a concept that opponents were quick to label "amnesty." Obama of course denies any talk of amnesty, saying instead that he wants illegal immigrants to pay penalties, pay taxes, learn English, and then go "to the back of the line."

Ed Krayewski, "5 Reasons to Grant Amnesty to Illegal Immigrants," Reason.com, February 7, 2013. Copyright © 2013 Reason Foundation. All rights reserved. Reproduced with permission.

But what's wrong with granting amnesty to hard-working, tax-paying individuals whose only crime is their immigration status? Indeed, amnesty is not only the best solution to our immigration problem, it is the *only* feasible solution. Here are five reasons to grant amnesty to illegal immigrants now.

Five Reasons to Grant Amnesty

1. Immigration Is Good for the Economy

For all the rhetoric about immigrants stealing jobs, immigration actually provides a benefit to the national economy, whether those immigrants crossed the border legally or not. Why? Because of what economists call the specialization of labor. As Jonathan Hoenig, proprietor of the *Capitalist Pig* blog, explains: "The fact that foreigners are eager to pick crops, clean houses, bus tables and produce allows more of us to afford cheaper food and better services, affording us even more wealth to enjoy and invest. It's not the immigrants, but the taxes, spending and entitlements (most of which immigrants don't even receive) that have drained the economy dry."

The vast majority [of illegal immigrants] want to stay in the country in order to work and so naturally steer clear of breaking any laws.

---

2. Illegal Immigrants Already Pay Taxes

One of President Obama's markers on the path to citizenship is "paying taxes," but most illegal immigrants already do so. As Reason Foundation Senior Analyst Shikha Dalmia has reported, in 2006 an estimated 8 million illegal immigrants—up to two thirds of the total—paid taxes, including both income taxes and Medicare and Social Security taxes. Indeed, revenue from illegal immigrants is estimated at $11 billion a year to Social Security alone, and there's not even a pretense of those payments leading to eventual benefits. And of course everyone who buys things in the U.S. pays sales taxes, irrespective of their immigration status. Undoubtedly, even more illegal immigrants would pay taxes if they didn't have to worry about possible deportation as a consequence.

3. Most Illegal Immigrants Are Otherwise Law-Abiding

While illegal immigration is a crime, the act of crossing the border without authorization is a mere misdemeanor. Immigrants, in fact, may help drive crime down. The vast majority want to stay in the country in order to work and so naturally steer clear of breaking any laws. And as The Future of Freedom Foundation's Sheldon Richman pointed out a few years ago, all manners of violent crimes dropped dramatically since 1986, the last time an amnesty was granted to illegal immigrants. Yes, 14 percent of federal inmates are illegal immigrants, but they are largely there for immigration violations. On the state level, Richman notes, less than 5 percent of inmates are illegal immigrants. Not exactly the makings of a crime wave.

4. Immigration Is a Natural Right

Last week, Judge Andrew Napolitano explained . . . at Reason.com that immigration is a natural right. What does that mean? A natural right is a right inherent to our humanity, and the freedom of movement is such a right. The idea that immigration needs to be "authorized" by the government flies in the face of that freedom. Immigrants who come to America seeking the opportunity to work and pursue happiness, or those brought here at too young an age to have any say in the matter, ought to be able to stay to pursue those opportunities. Conversely, employers ought to be able to enter into contracts with any would-be employees they please. The government doesn't own the country and political borders are just lines on maps. Treating law-abiding people like criminals simply because they didn't meet the bureaucratic requirements of migration abrogates their natural right to travel and Americans' natural right to freely associate and make contracts.

5. There Are Too Many Illegal Immigrants To Do Anything Else

According to the latest estimates, there are about 11 million illegal immigrants in America. That's a lot of people. It would be exceedingly difficult to deport them all—if not totally impossible. Indeed, even attempting to do so would require a massive expansion of government bureaucracy, particularly in the form of new government workers to round up illegal immigrants, process them, and deport them. The inhumanity of this approach goes without saying: Individuals would be ripped away from their families and communities. And there would also be dire economic consequences from removing millions of hard-working residents from the domestic labor pool.

It's time to face the facts: The millions of illegal immigrants currently residing in the United States are overwhelmingly law-abiding, tax-paying, and hard-working. Grant them amnesty and let them continue to make America a better place.

Organizations to Contact

The editors have compiled the following list of organizations concerned with the issues debated in this book. The descriptions are derived from materials provided by the organizations. All have publications or information available for interested readers. The list was compiled on the date of publication of the present volume; names, addresses, phone and fax numbers, and e-mail and Internet addresses may change. Be aware that many organizations take several weeks or longer to respond to inquiries, so allow as much time as possible.

American Civil Liberties Union (ACLU)
125 Broad St., 18th Floor, New York, NY   10004
(212) 549-2500
e-mail: infoaclu@aclu.org
website: www.aclu.org

The American Civil Liberties Union (ACLU) is a national organization that works to defend Americans' civil rights as guaranteed in the US Constitution. The ACLU Immigrants' Rights Project is dedicated to expanding and enforcing the civil liberties and civil rights of noncitizens, and to combating public and private discrimination against immigrants. The ACLU publishes the semiannual newsletter *Civil Liberties Alert*, as well as briefing papers, including the report *American Exile: Rapid Deportations That Bypass the Courtroom.*

American Immigration Control Foundation (AICF)
PO Box 525, Monterey, VA   24465
(540) 468-2022
website: www.aicfoundation.com

The American Immigration Control Foundation (AICF) is a nonpartisan organization that favors deportation of illegal immigrants and opposes amnesty and guest worker legislation. AICF works to inform American citizens of the disastrous effects of uncontrolled immigration. AICF publishes several books, videos, and reports on the topic of immigration, including the policy brief "Exposed: The Real Reason for Amnesty."

American Immigration Council
1331 G St. NW, Suite 200, Washington, DC 20005-3141
(202) 507-7500
website: www.americanimmigrationcouncil.org

The American Immigration Council is an educational organization that works to strengthen America by honoring its immigrant history. The organization promotes humane immigration policies that honor human rights and works to achieve fairness for immigrants under the law. It publishes numerous fact sheets and reports through its Immigration Policy Center, including "The President's Discretion, Immigration Enforcement, and the Rule of Law."

Center for American Progress
1333 H St. NW, 10th Floor, Washington, DC 20005
(202) 682-1611
website: www.americanprogress.org

The Center for American Progress is a nonprofit, nonpartisan organization dedicated to improving the lives of Americans through progressive ideas and action. The center dialogues with leaders, thinkers, and citizens to explore the vital issues facing America and the world. The organization publishes numerous research papers, which are available at its website, including "The Economic Case for a Clear, Quick Pathway to Citizenship."

Center for Immigration Studies (CIS)
1629 K St. NW, Suite 600, Washington, DC 20006
(202) 466-8185 • fax: (202) 466-8076
website: www.cis.org

The Center for Immigration Studies (CIS) is an independent research organization dedicated to providing immigration policy makers, the academic community, news media, and concerned citizens with reliable information about the social, economic, environmental, security, and fiscal consequences of legal and illegal immigration in the United States. CIS is interested in a unique "low-immigration, pro-immigrant" vision that seeks fewer immigrants but a warmer welcome for those admitted. The organization publishes reports and opinion pieces available at its website, including "President Obama's 'Deferred Action' Program for Illegal Aliens Is Plainly Unconstitutional."

Federation for American Immigration Reform (FAIR)

25 Massachusetts Ave. NW, Suite 330, Washington, DC   20001
(877) 627-3247 • fax: (202) 387-3447
website: www.fairus.org

The Federation for American Immigration Reform (FAIR) is a nonprofit organization of concerned citizens who share a common belief that the nation's immigration policies must be reformed to serve the national interest. FAIR seeks to improve border security, to stop illegal immigration and to promote immigration levels at rates of about 300,000 a year. FAIR publishes the monthly *Immigration Report* and other publications, including "Questions Everyone Should Ask About Executive Amnesty."

Migration Policy Institute (MPI)

1400 16th St. NW, Suite 300, Washington, DC   20036
(202) 266-1940 • fax: (202) 266-1900
e-mail: info@migrationpolicy.org
website: www.migrationpolicy.org

The Migration Policy Institute (MPI) is an independent, nonpartisan think tank dedicated to analysis of the movement of people worldwide. MPI provides analysis, development, and evaluation of migration and refugee policies at the local, national, and international levels. MPI publishes books, reports, and fact sheets, including the fact sheet "Major US Immigration Laws, 1790–Present."

National Council of La Raza (NCLR)

1126 16th St. NW, Suite 600, Washington, DC   20036
(202) 785-1670 • fax: (202) 776-1792
e-mail: comments@nclr.org
website: www.nclr.org

The National Council of La Raza (NCLR) is a Hispanic civil rights and advocacy organization that works to improve opportunities for Hispanic Americans. NCLR conducts applied research, policy analysis, and advocacy, providing a Latino perspective in five key areas, including civil rights and immigration. NCLR produces several publications, including the fact sheet "Voices Across America Support Administrative Relief."

National Immigration Forum

50 F St. NW, Suite 300, Washington, DC   20001
(202) 347-0040 • fax: (202) 347-0058
website: www.immigrationforum.org

The National Immigration Forum is an organization that advocates for the value of immigrants and immigration to the nation. The organization works to advance sound federal immigration solutions through policy expertise, communications outreach, and coalition building work. The National Immigration Forum publishes numerous backgrounders, fact sheets, and issue papers, including "America's Immigration System Undermines Competitiveness: Skilled Immigrants Must Be Welcomed."

National Immigration Law Center (NILC)

3435 Wilshire Blvd., Suite 2850, Los Angeles, CA   90010
(213) 639-3900 • fax: (213) 639-3911
e-mail: reply@nilc.org
website: www.nilc.org

The National Immigration Law Center (NILC) is dedicated to protecting and promoting the rights of low-income immigrants and their family members. NILC engages in policy advocacy, impact litigation, and education to secure fair treatment in the courts for immigrants, preserve a safety net for immigrants, and open opportunities for immigrants. NILC publishes briefing papers for policy makers, toolkits for immigration advocates, and materials used in its litigation.

National Network for Immigrant and Refugee Rights (NNIRR)

310 8th St., Suite 303, Oakland, CA   94607
(510) 465-1984 • fax: (510) 465-1885
e-mail: nnirrinfo@nnirr.org
website: www.nnirr.org

The National Network for Immigrant and Refugee Rights (NNIRR) is a national organization composed of local coalitions and immigrant, refugee, community, religious, civil rights, and labor organizations and activists. NNIRR works to promote a just immigration and refugee policy in the United States and to defend and expand the rights of all immigrants and refugees, regardless of immigration status. NNIRR publishes fact sheets and reports, including "10 Principles for Ensuring Fair and Humane Immigration Policy."

Negative Population Growth (NPG)

2861 Duke St., Suite 36, Alexandria, VA   22314
(703) 370-9510 • fax: (703) 370-9514
website: www.npg.org

Negative Population Growth (NPG) is an organization that aims to educate the American public and political leaders about the detrimental effects of overpopulation on the environment, resources, and quality of life. NPG advocates a smaller US population accomplished through reduced legal immigration rates and smaller families. NPG publishes a quarterly newsletter, *Population Perspectives*; a bimonthly journal, *NPG Journal*; and numerous forum papers, including "All in the Family: Preferences for Relatives Drive US Immigration and Population Growth."

NumbersUSA Action

1601 N Kent St., Suite 1100, Arlington, VA 22209
(703) 816-8820
website: www.numbersusa.com

NumbersUSA Action is an immigration-reduction organization. NumbersUSA aims to persuade public officials to support immigration policies that protect all Americans—especially the most vulnerable and including the foreign-born—from losing wages, taxes, individual freedoms, quality of life, and access to nature due to excessive immigration. Numbers-USA publishes fact sheets and articles at its website, including "Stop Amnesty."

US Citizenship and Immigration Services (USCIS)

425 I St. NW, Washington, DC 20536
(800) 375-5283
website: www.uscis.gov

US Citizenship and Immigration Services (USCIS), a government agency, oversees lawful immigration to the United States. USCIS provides immigration information, grants immigration and citizenship benefits, promotes an awareness and understanding of citizenship, and ensures the integrity of the US immigration system. USCIS provides information about immigration laws and recent reforms and publishes a blog, *The Beacon*.

US Immigration and Customs Enforcement (ICE)

500 12th St. SW, Washington, DC 20536
website: www.ice.gov

US Immigration and Customs Enforcement (ICE) is the principal investigative arm of the US Department of Homeland Security (DHS). ICE's primary mission is to promote homeland security and public safety through the criminal and civil enforcement of federal laws governing border control, customs, trade, and immigration. ICE publishes the quarterly *Cornerstone Report*, fact sheets, and reports.

Bibliography

Books

Deborah A. Boehm
Intimate Migrations: Gender, Family, and Illegality Among Transnational Mexicans. New York: New York University Press, 2012.

Joseph H. Carens
The Ethics of Immigration. New York: Oxford University Press, 2013.

Aviva Chomsky
Undocumented: How Immigration Became Illegal. Boston: Beacon Press, 2014.

Tanya Golash-Boza
Due Process Denied: Detentions and Deportations in the United States. New York: Routledge, 2012.

Alfonso Gonzales
Reform Without Justice: Latino Migrant Politics and the Homeland Security State. New York: Oxford University Press, 2014.

Samantha Hauptman
The Criminalization of Immigration: The Post 9/11 Moral Panic. El Paso, TX: LFB Scholarly Publishing, 2013.

Janet Levy
Illegal Immigration and Amnesty: Open Borders and National Security. New York: Rosen Publishing, 2010.

Taylor M. Lindall, ed.
Border Security and the Removal of Illegal Aliens. New York: Nova Science Publishers, 2011.

Sylvia Longmire | *Border Insecurity: Why Big Money, Fences, and Drones Aren't Making Us Safer.* New York: Palgrave Macmillan, 2014.

Eithne Luibhéid | *Pregnant on Arrival: Making the Illegal Immigrant.* Minneapolis: University of Minnesota Press, 2013.

Pilar Marrero | *Killing the American Dream: How Anti-Immigration Extremists Are Destroying the Nation.* New York: Palgrave Macmillan, 2012.

Anne McNevin | *Contesting Citizenship: Irregular Migrants and New Frontiers of the Political.* New York: Columbia University Press, 2011.

Deirdre M. Moloney | *National Insecurities: Immigrants and US Deportation Policy Since 1882.* Chapel Hill: University of North Carolina Press, 2012.

Mae M. Ngai | *Impossible Subjects: Illegal Aliens and the Making of Modern America.* Princeton, NJ: Princeton University Press, 2014.

Peter Schrag | *Not Fit for Our Society: Immigration and Nativism in America.* Berkeley: University of California Press, 2010.

Rogers M. Smith, ed. | *Citizenship, Borders, and Human Needs.* Philadelphia: University of Pennsylvania Press, 2011.

Richard M. Taylor
and Louis O.
Walker, eds.

*Border Security and Illegal
Immigration Enforcement.* New York:
Nova Science Publishers, 2012.

Daniel M.
Turcotte

*US Immigration: Key Trends, Policies,
and Programs.* New York: Nova
Science Publishers, 2013.

Periodicals and Internet Sources

American
Immigration
Control
Foundation

"The Case Against Amnesty," *Policy
Brief*, June 2013. www.aicfoundation
.com.

Doug Bandow

"Immigration Benefits the US, So
Let's Legalize All Work," *Forbes*,
September 16, 2013.

Michael Bargo Jr.

"Federal Enforcement, Not
Immigration Reform, Is Needed,"
American Thinker, May 4, 2013.

Jagdish Bhagwati
and Francisco
Rivera-Batiz

"A Kinder, Gentler Immigration
Policy," *Foreign Affairs*, vol. 92, no. 6,
November/December 2013.
www.foreignaffairs.com.

Aura Bogado

"Five Things to Know About
Immigration and Enforcement,"
Nation, February 20, 2013.

Ronald
Brownstein

"Why the Time Is Finally Right for
'Amnesty,'" *National Journal*, April 18,
2013.

Emily Chertoff

"Deport the Interlopers? But They've
Been Here All Along," *Atlantic*,
January 30, 2013.

Adam Davidson	"Do Immigrants Actually Hurt the US Economy?" *New York Times*, February 12, 2013
Jim DeMint and Robert Rector	"Amnesty for Illegal Immigrants Will Cost America," *Washington Post*, May 6, 2013.
Jon Feere	"Is the 'Kids Act' Amnesty Really Just for Kids? Probably Not," Center for Immigration Studies, February 2014. www.cis.org.
Marshall Fitz	"Piecemeal Immigration Proposals Miss the Point: A Path to Citizenship Is a Political and Policy Imperative," Center for American Progress, December 11, 2012. www.americanprogress.org.
Conor Friedersdorf	"The Thorny Issue of Illegal Immigration and the Rule of Law," *Atlantic*, August 5, 2011.
Juan Carlos Guzmán and Raúl C. Jara	"The Economic Benefits of Passing the DREAM Act," Center for American Progress, October 2012. www.americanprogress.org.
William P. Hoar	"Lawmakers Advocate Amnesty for 11 Million Lawbreakers," *New American*, June 3, 2013.

Immigration
Policy Center

"The Fallacy of 'Enforcement First':
Immigration Enforcement Without
Immigration Reform Has Been
Failing for Decades," American
Immigration Council, May 2013.
www.immigrationpolicy.org.

Fawn Johnson

"Immigration Dreams Become
Reality, Finally," *National Journal*,
June 15, 2012.

Mark Krikorian

"Enforcement, then Amnesty, on
Immigration," *National Review*, vol.
66, no. 2, February 10, 2014.

Robert Lynch and
Patrick Oakford

"The Economic Effects of Granting
Legal Status and Citizenship to
Undocumented Immigrants," Center
for American Progress, March 20,
2013. www.americanprogress.org.

Warren Mass

"Permanent Amnesty, Temporary
Border," *New American*, April 8, 2013.

Christopher
Matthews

"The Economics of Immigration:
Who Wins, Who Loses, and Why,"
Time, January 30, 2013.

Ira Mehlman

"Five Moral Arguments Against the
DREAM Act," Townhall.com, July 1,
2011. www.townhall.com.

David North

"'You Can't Deport 11 Million
People' Statement Reflects Mistaken
Image," Center for Immigration
Studies *Backgrounder*, March 2013.
www.cis.org.

Pia M. Orrenius and Madeline Zavodny
"The Economic Consequences of Amnesty for Unauthorized Immigrants," *Cato Journal*, Winter 2012.

Eric Posner
"There's No Such Thing as an Illegal Immigrant," *Slate*, February 4, 2013. www.slate.com.

Robert Schlesinger
"The Unilateral Presidency," *U.S. News & World Report*, November 21, 2014.

Peter Skerry
"Splitting the Difference on Illegal Immigration," *National Affairs*, Winter 2013.

Irwin M. Stelzer
"The Perils of Reform," *Weekly Standard*, vol. 18, no. 23, February 25, 2013.

Cesar Vargas
"Don't End My American DREAM," *Politico*, July 23, 2013. www.politico.com.

Lorraine Woellert
"Amnesty for Illegal Immigrants Has Economic Benefits," *Bloomberg*, March 14, 2013. www.bloomberg.com.

Index

A

Administrative efficiency principle in legalization program, 43–44

Affordability principle in legalization program, 41–42

Alien Contract Labor Law, 83

American Dream, 73

American Federation of Labor and Congress of Industrial Organizations (AFL-CIO), 83

American Immigration Control Foundation, 45–55

American University, 79

Amnesty
disadvantages of, 45–55
fear of, 20
federal immigration workers, 52–53
as harmful, 48–49
illegal immigration and, 56–59
immigration reform and, 93–96
introduction, 8–9
by Obama, Barack, 53–55, 57–58
overpopulation/environmental concerns, 51–52
overview, 45–46
politics and money, 46–48
reasons to grant, 94–96
support for, 85
US fiscal problems, 50–51
US worker impact, 49

See also Legalization program; Pathway to citizenship/legal status

Anderson, Stuart, 63

Aneja, Abhay, 9

Application period length, 40

Applied Research Center, 34

Arizona v. United States, 27

B

Boehner, John, 31

Border Security, Economic Opportunity and Immigration Modernization Act, 36

Bush, George H.W., 33

Bush, George W., 14, 19, 32–33

C

Camarota, Steven A., 50

Capitalist Pig blog, 94

Capps, Randy, 66

Carson, Ben, 89–92

Center for American Progress (CAP), 9, 68–69

Center for Immigration Studies, 8, 50–51, 63–66, 68

Chemerinsky, Erwin, 31–34

Child inclusion in legalization program, 39

China, 12

Christian Science Monitor newspaper, 86–88

Clinton, Bill, 33

Complementary process principle
  in legalization program, 44
Congressional Budget Office, 50
Controlled Substance Act, 32
Creamer, Robert, 46–47
Criteria for qualifying, 40–41
Current Population Survey
  (March 2010), 67

D

Deferred Action for Childhood
  Arrivals (DACA), 29, 57
Deportation
    executive action and, 18–19
    Hispanics, 11, 13–15
    limitation of, 33
    overview, 10–11, 14
Disenfranchisement, 76
Documentary requirements, 38–39
DREAM (Development, Relief,
  and Education for Alien Minors)
  Act, 24, 62, 83

E

Edmonston, Barry, 65
Einstein, Albert, 75–76
El Salvador, 12, 58
English-language classes, 71
English-language skills, 37
Environmental concerns, 51–52,
  73–76
Eschbach, Karl, 57
Executive action on immigrants
    authority over domestic af-
      fairs, 25–26
    dangers of, 24–30
    debate over, 21–22
    deportation, 18–19

duty to enforce law, 27–29
    legal precedent, 26–27
    need for, 16–17
    by Obama, Barack, 16–23
    overview, 24–25
    as temporary solution, 20–21
    unpassed bill on, 17–18

F

Federal immigration workers,
  52–53
Federation for American Immigra-
  tion Reform (FAIR), 68–72
Fitz, Marshall, 60–67
Fix, Michael, 66, 67
Foster, David, 73–76
Frank, Barney, 85
Frankfurter, Felix, 30
Free and reduced-price school
  lunches, 66
Freedom of Information Act, 58
Future of Freedom Foundation, 95

G

General Accountability Office
  (GAO), 55
Google Hangout session, 25
Great Recession, 12
Green economy, 73–76
Gross domestic product (GDP),
  61, 69
Guatemala, 12, 58
Guest-worker program, 89–92
Guzmán, Juan Carlos, 62

H

Hanen, Andrew S., 56, 59
Hawley, George, 48

Henderson, Everett, 66
Heritage Foundation, 50, 63, 68
Hines v. Davidowitz, 33
Hinojosa-Ojeda, Raúl, 61–62, 69,
71–72
Hispanics, 11, 13–15, 48
Hoenig, Jonathan, 94
Honduras, 12, 58

I

Illegal aliens, 69–70
Illegal immigrants/immigration
amnesty and, 56–59, 83
border crossings, 17
debate over, 79, 81, 82
impact of, 50
increase in, 70
as law-abiding, 95
number of, 96
path to citizenship, 84–85, 86
as tax payers, 94–95
See also Unauthorized immigrants
Immigrants/immigration
application period length, 40
documentary requirements,
38–39
federal immigration workers,
52–53
guest-worker program, 89–92
legal permanent residents, 62
Mexican-origin immigrants,
79–80
minimum wage concerns, 74
naturalized citizens, 7, 62
overpopulation concerns,
51–52
overtime laws, 74
permanent noncitizen residency, 77–80

temporary residence status, 7,
40–41
unaccompanied alien minors,
58
See also Executive action on
immigrants; Unauthorized
immigrants
Immigration Act (1965), 10
Immigration and Nationality Act
(1952), 28
Immigration and Naturalization
Service (INS), 29, 35, 42
*Immigration and Naturalization
Service v. Chadha*, 27
Immigration Law Reform Institute, 58
Immigration reform
amnesty and, 93–96
debate over, 75
guest-worker program, 89–92
introduction, 7–9
pathway to citizenship and,
77–81, 86–88
See also Amnesty; Legalization
program; Pathway to
citizenship/legal status
Immigration Reform and Control
Act (IRCA) (1986), 7–8, 36, 44,
69, 84
Immigrations and Customs Enforcement (ICE), 34, 54
Impoundment Control Act (1974),
27
Inclusion principle in legalization
program, 37–41
India, 12
INS v. Lennon, 34
Intergovernmental Panel on Climate Change (IPCC), 74

Internal Revenue Service, 87
International Red Cross, 74

J

Jara, Raúl, 62

K

Hurricane Katrina, 75
Kavanaugh, Brett, 32
Kleiner, Sam, 31–34
Krayewski, Ed, 93–96
Krikorian, Mark, 82–85

L

Labor movement, 83
Latinos, 14–15
See also Hispanics
Legalization program
   administrative efficiency prin-
    ciple, 43–44
   affordability principle, 41–42
   complementary process prin-
    ciple, 44
   crafting of, 35–44
   economic benefit, 60–67, 94
   economic burden, 68–72
   inclusion principle, 37–41
   mere legalization proposal,
    78–80
   overview, 35–36, 60–61
   past recipients, 70–72
   safety principle, 42–43
   simplicity principle, 36–37
   snapshot accounting, 63–67
   See also Amnesty
Legal permanent residents, 62
Lennon, John, 34

M

Malcolm, John G., 24–30
Marshall, John, 32
Mass legalization. *See* Amnesty
McCain, John, 48
McConnell, Mitch, 31
Medicare, 50, 64, 65, 67, 94
Medina, Eliseo, 85
Meese, Edwin, 54
Meissner, Doris, 29
Mere legalization proposal, 78–80
Mexican Consulate, 75
Mexican-origin immigrants, 79–80
Mexico, 11–12
Migration Policy Institute, 58
Minimum wage concerns, 74
Motomura, Hiroshi, 80

N

Napolitano, Andrew, 95
Napolitano, Janet, 54–55
National Affairs journal, 83, 84
National Council of La Raza, 25
National Foundation for American
  Policy, 63
National Journal, 48
Naturalized citizens, 7, 62
Nixon, Richard, 26–27
North, David, 8

O

Oakford, Patrick, 60–67
Obama, Barack and immigration
  amnesty and, 45, 53–55,
   57–58
  deportations, 10–11, 14

immigration reform, 86, 90, 93
legal support for, 31–34
mere legalization proposal, 79
path to citizenship, 94
See also Executive action on immigrants
Obamacare, 50
Office of Legal Counsel, 28
Overpopulation concerns, 51–52
Overtime laws, 74

P

Passel, Jeffrey, 67
Pastor, Manuel, 62
Pathway to citizenship/legal status
debate over, 82–85
green economy, 73–76
as harmful, 48
immigration reform, 77–81, 86–88
permanent noncitizen residency, 77–80
public opinion of, 13
See also Amnesty
Patient Protection and Affordable Care Act. *See* Obamacare
Permanent noncitizen residency, 77–80
Permanent residence status, 7
Pew Hispanic Center, 48, 64
Pew Research Center, 10–15
Philippines, 12

R

Reagan, Ronald, 7–8, 33, 79–80
Reason.com, 95
Rector, Robert, 50, 63–65
Richman, Sheldon, 95

Roney, Lisa S., 35–44
Roosevelt, Theodore, 73
Rubio, Marco, 83
Rule of law, 92

S

Safety principle in legalization program, 42–43
Hurricane Sandy, 75
Senate Budget Committee, 50
Service Employees International Union, 83
Silva, Astrid, 22–23
Simplicity principle in legalization program, 36–37
Skerry, Peter, 77–81, 84
Smith, Ian, 56–59
Smith, James P., 65
Smith, Lamar, 54
Social Security, 50, 64, 65, 67, 94
Social Security Trust Fund, 61, 63
Spouse inclusion in legalization program, 39
Stand Up Straight: How Progressives Can Win (Creamer), 47
Supplemental Security Income (SSI), 50

T

Temporary Assistance to Needy Families (TANF), 50
Temporary residence status, 7, 40–41
Thompson, Elihu, 76
Train v. City of New York, 26

U

Unaccompanied alien minors (UAMs), 58
Unauthorized immigrants
green economy and, 73–76
introduction, 7–9
mass legalization disadvantages, 45–55
public perception of, 10–15
severe weather concerns, 75
tax payments by, 62–63
See also Illegal immigrants/immigration
United States v. Nixon, 32
University of California, Los Angeles (UCLA), 69, 80
University of Houston, 48
US Chamber of Commerce, 47, 83

US Department of Health and Human Services, 58
US Department of Homeland Security (DHS), 14, 35, 54
US Department of Justice, 28, 32

W

Wall Street Journal newspaper, 47
Washington Post newspaper, 58
Wolgin, Philip E., 9, 60–67
Women, Infants and Children food program (WIC), 50

Y

Youngstown Sheet & Tube Co. v. Sawyer, 26